T5-AFK-583

Gay and Lesbian Politics

Gay and Lesbian Politics

Sexuality and the Emergence of a New Ethic

Mark Blasius

Temple University Press
Philadelphia

Temple University Press, Philadelphia 19122

Published 1994
Printed in the United States of America

The paper used in this publication meets the minimum requirements of American National Standard for Information Sciences—Permanence of Paper for Printed Library Materials, ANSI Z39.48-1984 ♾

Library of Congress Cataloging-in-Publication Data

Blasius, Mark.
Gay and lesbian politics : sexuality and the emergence of a new ethic / Mark Blasius.
p. cm.
Includes bibliographical references and index.
ISBN 1-56639-173-3 (alk. paper). — ISBN 1-56639-174-1 (pbk : alk. paper)
1. Homosexuality—Political aspects—United States. 2. Lesbianism—Political aspects—United States. 3. Gay men—United States—Political activity. 4. Lesbians—United States—Political activity. I. Title.
HQ76.3.U5B56 1994
305.9'0664—dc20 93-40681

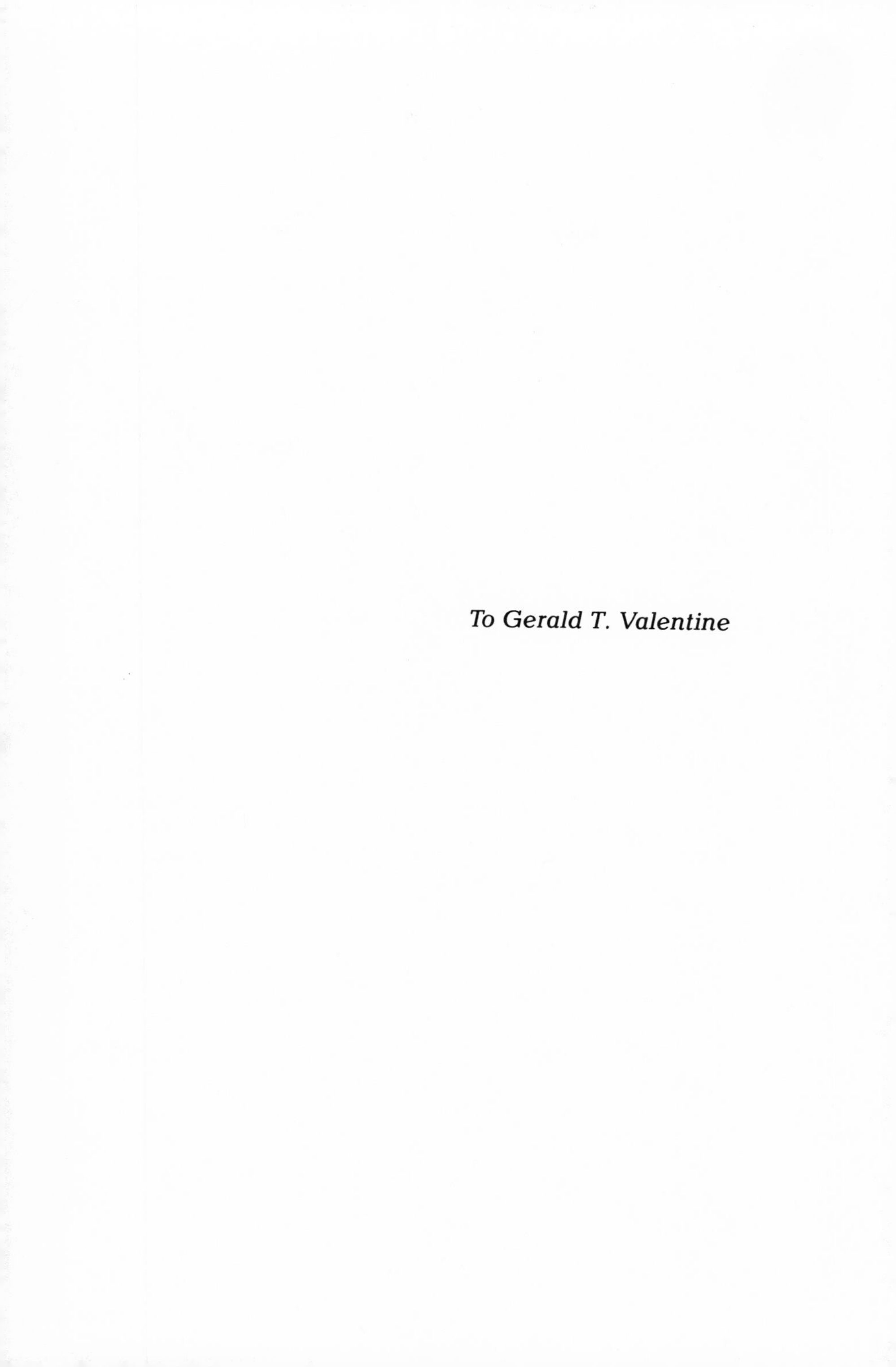

To Gerald T. Valentine

Contents

Acknowledgments

This is my attempt to theorize in a general but comprehensive way contemporary gay and lesbian politics. Earlier versions of this work were shaped by comments from Richard Falk, Michel Foucault, Jennifer Hochschild, George Kateb, Anne Norton, and Tracy Strong.

Individual chapters of this book were presented under the auspices of the Gay and Lesbian Caucus of the American Political Science Association, the North American Society for Social Philosophy, and lesbian, gay, and queer studies gatherings at Columbia, Yale, and Harvard Universities and at the University of Toronto. They were helpfully commented upon by Juanita Ramos Diaz-Cotto, Dennis Fischman, Cheryl Hall, Harry Hirsch, Melissa Orlie, Shane Phelan, and Sarah Slavin.

The Center for Lesbian and Gay Studies at the City University of New York, especially its monthly research colloquium, provided crucial intellectual sustenance for my work. I was nourished by a community of lesbian and gay scholars who set standards of discourse for me and enabled me to be openly gay in my professional life. Without that support this book might never have been written. I was also assisted by the understanding of my colleagues at CUNY-LaGuardia, particularly my chairperson, Lily Shohat, by a PSC-CUNY Faculty Research Award, and by LaGuardia's Publication Office (especially Bill Freeland) in preparing the figures.

Friends have helped me along, too. While I was writing the final version of this book, the glamorous Odell Mays analyzed, refracted, and led me to clarify Chapter 1; he also provided moral support when times were rough, as did Candida Scott Piel. Daniel Defert remained a faithful and encouraging friend before and during the illness of, and after the death of his lover, Michel Foucault. In continuing to share political and intellectual work with me, Daniel introduced me to Yves Roussel, who provided a useful perspective on Chapter 2. Guy Hocquenghem, Dennis Altman, and Michel Cressole suggested by word or example that I begin this project. My neighbor Doric Wilson rapidly and expertly prepared the index. Debby Stuart was an excellent production editor. Finally, of all of my friends, Michael Denneny deserves the most gratitude. For years, while working out with me in the Chelsea Gym and accompanying me all over New York City and Fire Island, he egged me on, gently but definitively criticized my ideas, and reminded me how long I was taking.

A final acknowledgment is to the other gay men

and lesbians who have written and are writing about the character of the lives we are living. I am convinced that what we are doing is something historically new, an experiment in living that must to be recorded whether it be through art, theoretical and practical reflection, or biography, so others can learn from and build upon our experiences, including our loss through the holocaust that is AIDS.

Gay and Lesbian Politics

Introduction

This book is about how gay men and lesbians have made sexuality a political issue in our time. The phenomenon it describes is quintessentially political; therefore, analyzing it goes to the heart of what politics is today. Being lesbian or gay today is by definition political: regardless of one's sexual practices one must choose to become gay or lesbian by "coming out" subjectively and interpersonally; by fitting oneself into extant social relationships *as* gay or lesbian (with all that this entails in terms of power relationships—the possibility of retaliation, as well as the possibility of leadership, of being a role model for others); and by establishing a relationship between oneself and other lesbians and gay men through what has come to be called the lesbian and gay community—by being "in the life," as black gay men historically phrased it. Of course, one can be a person who has sex with someone of the same sex but does not identify oneself as gay or lesbian. Such a person exists in the prepolitical condition of domination within a society that privileges heterosexuality, and he or she accommodates this by "passing" as heterosexual—by being unable or unwilling to eliminate the domination. Indeed, considering the normative language that has described homosexuality in Western culture—all of which consigns it to what cannot be spoken about, seen, or heard, that is, to what cannot exist—perhaps "prepolitical" is too weak a description of the phenomenon of the closet. The ontological status of such a person who has sex with people of the same sex is problematical in a fundamental sense. Not only have homoerotic activities been subject to historical erasure and contemporary censure, but the person who habitually engages in such activities, "the homosexual," tends to be denied the right to exist as such. For example, those in the U.S. military currently can exist there only so long as they do not exist *as* gay or lesbian, that is, do not identify themselves as such.

To be sure, having sexual relationships with someone of the same sex has not, either historically or culturally, had the *political* significance it does here and now. (Indeed, there is great scholarly debate about whether people in other cultures and times who have or had sexual relationships with others of the same sex can be said to form a distinctive social group, with or without self-identification as such, based upon their same-sex sexual relationships.) The way power has come to be exercised in contemporary societies, through sexuality as I analyze it in this book, is the historical condition of possibility for a *politics* of sexuality. Lesbians and gay men are the principal subjects of such a politics.

In politicizing sexuality, lesbians and gay men have contested how they have been socially constructed as pathological. This is political because such construction occurs through a shaping of individual subjective and interpersonal identity by recourse to a structure of power relations within society. In demonstrating how cultural norms, social institutions, as well as laws are instances of systemic domination—as conventions through which some people can exercise power over other people—the lesbian and gay movement has produced "truth," knowledge about politics today. But this movement has itself only become possible to the extent that lesbians and gay men have identified themselves with each other. Through the emergence of what I call a lesbian and gay ethos, a way of life more encompassing than either a sexual orientation or a lifestyle, one shares values and an interpretation of reality with others as a consequence of one's personal choice to come out, to challenge the "truth" of the pathological label "homosexual" and become "gay" or "lesbian." In this way, one constitutes oneself as an ethical subject that can then allow for a collective recognition of and challenge to domination.

Obviously, there is more to contemporary lesbian and gay existence than a political movement. There is an expanding lesbian and gay culture, understood in the broadest sense to include the arts and literature, scholarship, religious institutions, and athletic leagues, for example. There are, as well, formal groups and informal networks of individuals devoted to a multitudinous variety of pursuits that are not "political" in the narrow sense of concern with the formal structures of power in our society. Indeed, many lesbians and gays would consider themselves apolitical, particularly if "political" is defined solely as participating in a lesbian or gay organization. However, the act of "coming out" to nongays and to other lesbians and gays is itself political (even if one is not a joiner of organizations) since, as I demonstrate, it challenges the coerced conformity, the cultural invisibility, of men who have sex with men and of women who have sex with women and provides the basis in individual ethics for politics. Moreover, besides the work of the explicitly political organizations, most of lesbian and gay culture is at the same time "cultural politics," the activity of calling into question and transforming the power relations that condition how sexuality is conceptualized, represented, and expressed behaviorally at the present time. Thus, there is scholarship that wrests facts about homosexuality from methodological oblivion or outright censorship and institutionalizes these facts as an educational canon. Homoerotic and activist visual art create new sources of information about sexuality that extant media and their economic sponsors resist. Lesbian and gay sports call into question power relations articulated through gender, as well as the separation of athletics from erotics. Lesbian and gay spirituality problematizes dominant sources of personal meaning and practices for the reinforcement and transmission to others of that meaning within everyday life. And lesbian and gay literature, fictional and nonfictional, provides indigenous accounts of existence in opposition to those of experts whose narratives are informed by the position they occupy in structures of power that dominate lesbians and gays.

Nevertheless, some lesbians view the concept "lesbian and gay community" as problematic. Because they conceive their erotic (and many of their political) interests as being exclusively with other women and often opposed to those of men, the "lesbian" in the lesbian and gay community might only mean a temporary coalition of expedience and efficacy with gay men for specific programmatic goals. Some gay men, too, view lesbian feminists as moralistic in sexual matters. To be sure, both gay men and lesbians tend to seek erotic (and, to varying degrees, nonerotic) separatism. However, when they do work together beyond fighting an immediate and common enemy—where they do not "have" to exist together, the possibility of voluntary community (the creation of "safe space" and friendship between them) a common way of life or ethos comes into being.

Furthermore, lesbian and gay people of color often feel excluded because they perceive that the "community" reproduces the patterns of prejudice and discrimination based upon ethnicity, race, and class present in the larger society. Indeed, people of color understandably are sometimes reluctant to trade the social risks of coming out for doing so into a "community" that reproduces internally those social inequalities. Such patterns of exclusion therefore undermine the possibility of collective identity and any attempts based upon it to eliminate oppression of gays and lesbians. The voices of the lived experience of color, ethnicity, and class in lesbian and gay life must be listened to by interpreters of that life, must be incorporated into any emerging canon, and, perhaps most important, must contribute to any theoretical discourse that analyzes the sources of and helps catalyze a collective identity and politics.

The perspective here is not primarily that of a category of subjective identity (the author's lived experience as a gay man of middle-class European American ancestry—although it has obviously been informed by it). Rather, I have tried to *create* perspective from the analytical category of *sexuality:* one that applies to all lesbians and gay men regardless of other differences (although these other differences affect how lesbians and gays experience sexuality, affect how they make a political issue of it, and hence must inform any analysis of the politics of sexuality). Sexuality is, to be sure, a category of personal experience. But, more specifically and more important, it is a lifelong *problem* for lesbians and gay men—not having been raised to be lesbian or gay, as soon as they recognize their erotic desire for the same sex they must account for it. It is on this basis that the possibility of a lesbian and gay community can exist. Because sexuality is a basic existential issue for them, and because of the role sexuality plays in the exercise of power in our society, it becomes a political problem for which lesbians and gay men (among other people) have sought various political solutions.

Thus, lesbians and gay men are such because they have not been able to take their sexuality for granted. The fact of their respective sexual identities means that at some point in their lives they had to ask questions about and act based upon their own experience of sexuality, one different from what the culture's agents of socialization present to them as desirable. This problem usually begins to pose itself at a very early age; depending upon how one resolves it, one will become lesbian or gay sooner, later, or never. Persisting in one's erotic expression and finding others like oneself is a personal problem in a society that disallows or actively represses such expression. It becomes a political problem when those so hindered recognize their commonality and work together not only to eliminate the ways in which these relationships are disallowed but also to claim a right to have such relationships socially recognized and sanctioned. Further (and in order to do so), they must turn a given into an open question for which they provide the answer with the example of their own lives. That is, they must respond to the culturally defined problem of their existence by making it into something different in the order of truth. In the contemporary world, this is done through the act of public acknowledgment, "coming out," as authors of the despised acts; such acknowledgment both creates political agency that challenges power relations in society whose efficacy derives from their claim to truth and establishes the challenge as coming from political subjects on behalf of truth. This is why a significant part of the contemporary politics of homosexuality relies upon the production of truth (in literature, social-scientific knowledge, ethics and the self-help genre, etc.). The problem for those who have sex with people of the same sex is to insert into society's "regime of truth"—its procedures for producing, distributing, and regulating statements to the effect "this is how things are"—an account of their own sexual experience, since it is on the basis of the truth status of such experience that they have been oppressed.

It is my project here to analyze how such a politics of sexuality has historically come into being and how such a politics contributes both to our understanding of what politics is and to our understanding of the world in which we live. The first chapter is about how to understand, methodologically, lesbian and gay politics. In Chapter 2, I examine how such a politics of sexuality has become historically possible and locate lesbian and gay politics in relation to other ways in which sexuality has become a political issue in order to sharpen my analysis. In Chapter 3, I demonstrate how homoerotic practices allow for an individual and collective identity and thus a basis for a political movement. In Chapter 4, I discuss the principal political goals of the lesbian and gay movement through analysis of the rights it has asserted. Finally, in Chapter 5, I examine the effect lesbian and gay politics has had in the order of truth: a new ethic emerging from the use of sexuality in constituting oneself as an agent of one's actions; the consequent relations that coalesce to form an ethos that has both personal and political dimensions; and how this ethos transforms what we conceive politics to be today.

Chapter 1

The Creation of Gay and Lesbian Politics

crackers are born with the right to
be alive
i'm making ours up right here in yr face
Ntozake Shange

How is "sexuality" "political"? I place the two terms within quotation marks to indicate the definitional difficulties that must be addressed before the question can be answered. Our cultural preconceptions of what sexuality is and of what politics is may make the terms appear antithetical and an answer to the question seem inapparent if not impossible. Even participants in the U.S. lesbian and gay movement, at the forefront of what might be called "the politics of sexuality," often advocate as a tactical move a constitutional right to privacy within which intimate sexual relationships can be protected from government intrusion. Yet, as I argue in Chapter 2 ("sexuality" is defined more fully there), sexual practices have never been immune from political scrutiny and even intervention, and contemporary sexuality is a principal method through which modern forms of governmental power achieve (or find obstacles to the achievement of) their goals. Sexuality is both a site at which power is exercised and a method through which individuals constitute themselves as political subjects: sexuality is political.

In this chapter, however, I preface my analysis of sexuality as a political issue with a methodological discussion of how it can be conceptualized as such. I do this, first, not to sidestep the question of the nature of politics, but to ground this nature in today's historical reality; hence, a historical ontology of politics. I do so, second, because this conceptualization of politics allows for the development of the necessary methodological tools to analyze sexuality politically.

A Historical Ontology of Politics

Of note at the outset of my analysis are two characteristics of contemporary political life. They are notable whether politics is identified with the state's management of variables affecting the security, welfare, and prosperity of the citizenry or whether it is identified with the claims of social movements (from both Left and Right—witness the abortion debate in the United States). These characteristics are, first, in what way "the personal is political," meaning that the subjective choices of individuals can become collective political concerns and that subjectivity itself can be shaped by governmental agencies acting on behalf of collective concerns. The second characteristic is in what way "everything is political," that is, how any aspect of contemporary life (ranging from the use of fetal tissue to whether date rape has occurred, for example) can become a political issue.

First, we have on one side the management of subjectivity: when government agencies identify a mother as "negligent" for not choosing to undergo antenatal testing or abort a fetus that, say, is genetically "deficient" or that may develop AIDS; when government tries to create and foster families or households (through casework and welfare); or when government creates personal identity (through campaigns to "Americanize" immigrants or make Communists out of Russians). On the other side of the same coin, people resist such intervention through arguments for the irreducibility of personal choice, through the creation of nontraditional families and domestic partnerships, and through affirming cultural, racial, gender, and sexual identities that supersede national identity, for example.

Second, what becomes a political issue can be determined by the exigencies of governing, by emancipatory movements' analysis of oppressive power exercised within daily living and their calling for a politics of everyday life, and even by the creation of politics by negation. In this last case, some aspect of life may be designated by government authorities or social movements to be *not* political, often with a consequent politicization by other groups claiming that it *is* political. (This occurs, for example, when homophobic public figures are "outed," and when advocates of compulsory HIV [human immunodeficiency virus] testing, and tatooing of those who test positive, say that their concern is medical or hygienic, not political, to which affected groups respond that the motivation and consequence of such testing is political.) Given these uses of "political," what are the limits on what we can conceive politics to be before falling into totalitarianism or straining our use of the term "politics" toward incoherence?

One manner of responding to these questions might be to answer from within the framework of a tradition of thought relying upon a transhistorical understanding of politics; another might be to argue deductively from an a priori conceptualization of "the political." The former approach might posit the notion of a "tradition" founded by Aristotle. Here, politics would derive from the *polis*, the most comprehensive of human associations, which aims at human perfection (or at least fulfillment) and which finds its historical culmination in the modern state. In this approach, politics is about the state, as is the study of politics—political theory or political science; because the state is the most comprehensive human association, this is the master science in studying human affairs.[1] The latter approach might follow that of Bertrand Russell, claiming that power is "the fundamental concept in social science . . . in the same sense in which Energy is the fundamental concept in physics."[2] Here, the study of *power* is the master science in examining human reality. No matter whether it is exercised through

1. Aristotle, *The Politics of Aristotle*, ed. and trans. Ernest Barker (Oxford: Oxford University Press, 1958), 1.2.1252b9–1253a9, and *Nichomachean Ethics*, trans. Martin Ostwald (Indianapolis: Bobbs-Merrill, 1962), 1.2.1094a25–1094b.

2. Bertrand Russell, *Power: A New Social Analysis* (New York: W. W. Norton, 1938), 12–13, at 12.

economic, legal, military, or interpersonal relationships, all are manifestations of a desire, ostensibly rooted in human nature, for power. Politics, in this approach, would presumably be defined as the competitive struggle among desiring individuals (or groups) to exercise quantifiable power over others. Yet, the first idea, that politics is about people's aspirations for fulfillment or about attaining "the good" through the state or state-related agencies, neglects at the very least contemporary usages of politics in domains of human life relatively unconnected with the direct exercise of state power ("gender politics" in the workplace, the "politics" of agenda setting in organizations). Furthermore, the "common good" is not necessarily a motive for politics, as interest-group theory has it; when it is, it may be suspect, as the Marxist critique of ideology has it. Even the more "realist" second approach, which sees in human nature a desire for power that must be or is checked and balanced by other actors vying for power, fails to consider that such desire is itself historically and culturally constructed in individuals.

Instead of either of these approaches, I take as a starting point for conceptualizing politics simply "what happens in politics"—how it is historically and nominalistically constituted. What must politics be in order for it to be everywhere, for the personal to become political, for people to call their everybody life experience "political"? To say this is to conceptualize politics as a potentiality that inheres in social life. Politics "happens" when people join with each other to target how social life is organized (and to target specific social relations) for scrutiny and possible change.

This presupposes that such relations *can* be changed—that they are arbitrary rather than natural, divinely sanctioned, or the product of rational necessity. They are then called "political," and this targeting for analysis and possible change is "politics." Thus, what happens in politics is that people identify themselves with each other as a movement or collective "we" and problematize social relations within which they are enmeshed on behalf of the "politicalness" of these relations—that they are arbitrary human artifices and amenable to change, that they are *power* relations. (Contrary to Russell's analysis, these relations are not a priori political; they become so only to the extent that they are recognized and labeled as such.)

Why is politics about power relations? (Politics is *primarily* about power as distinct from, say, economic relations or technological capacity, which may be a resource for exercising power, or relations of communication, which might enable consent or agreement to power relations, even though politics is concerned with these secondarily, to the extent that they effect power relations.) As I indicate in the rest of this chapter, politics is about power: first, because human reality at any given time—both people's actions and their understandings of who they are based upon authorship of those actions—is constituted *through* relations with others—power relations (what I call "normativity," which can be institutionalized to a greater or lesser extent as "government"); second, because people in their freedom to act resist how their actions are determined by others and thus *change* that normativity—the procedures through which someone comes to know oneself and through which one's actions are able to be controlled by others; and, finally, politics is about power because people determine, albeit provisionally, what domains of life will be objectified for collective concern and the operation of power relations and what will not be—and then call this former domain "political," thus defining a *limit* to politics that is *historical.*

Thus, a historical ontology of politics is a recognition and questioning of, at once: (1) one's relation to oneself in subjectivity and an identity that makes possible one's relationships to others; (2) one's relation to others as mediated through collective norms, laws, institutions, and an experimentation with types of normativity; and (3) one's relation to truth by objectifying one's relation to oneself and to others which may have been previously understood as a given, *now* as produced through historically constructed and socioculturally contingent relations of power—that is, critical reflection upon one's relation to oneself and one's relation to others as "political." As such a historical ontology of politics, it is more appropriate to speak of a *politicization* of various aspects of contemporary life by social movements and even "schools of thought" to the extent that they have an effect on government policies (as, for example, "liberalism" did beginning in the nineteenth century, as "feminism" does now). I examine the politicization of sexuality, indeed, the creation of politics by the lesbian and gay movement in that social relations that had been perceived to be nonpolitical are now understood as political. (Relations constituting what are called "sexuality" that were formerly viewed as natural, divinely sanctioned, or of rational necessity are now, because of this politicization—a politics of sexuality by the lesbian and gay movement—viewed as produced by power relations that have been historically constructed and are therefore amenable to change.)

The analysis of lesbian and gay politics in this book shows how politics is created: (1) through a relation to oneself as having a lesbian or gay "sexual identity," thus making possible a lesbian and gay movement; (2) through a recognition with others that sexual practices, norms, and institutions are supported by a wider structure of power relations in society and are consequently subject to change by using the movement as a resource for doing so; and (3) through discourse about how what sexuality is conceived to be, its value, and the use of sexuality in living one's life are politically significant. All of these elements effect changes in contemporary relations of power that affect lesbian and gay people, and, indirectly, nongay people as well.

My starting point for analyzing lesbian and gay politics, as an identification and critique of the power relations that, through sexuality, are constitutive of modern life, involves answering three questions. To these *ontological* questions I provide answers that are *historically* specific, as exemplified in lesbian and gay politics: (1) How is power exercised today? Power is exercised such that people "have" a sexuality and are regulated—and "self-regulate"—through it; (2) What is at stake in power relations—why do people call them into question in politics? Lesbians and gays resist power so exercised through sexuality as an expression of an irreducible principle of freedom—in their case, freedom to *become individual* through erotic relations with others; (3) Why is power exercised this way? The power relations that constitute lesbian and gay oppression have been historically constituted by recourse to truth; hence, a central feature of lesbian and gay politics is a politicization of the truth claims on behalf of which power is exercised through sexuality. Historical specificity is theoretically requisite; thus, these questions and answers will enable me to develop the methodological tools for politically theorizing (homo and hetero) sexuality.

Power, Subjectivity, and Truth

Power: Heterosexist Domination, Homophobic Subjection

The term "power" describes a relationship between the actions of individuals or collectivities where the actions of one establish conditions for, shape in an ongoing way, or elicit possible actions of, the other. Power is a relation not simply among agents but among actions, and exercising power is a way of acting upon actions, guiding or organizing present conduct as well as behavior that might occur in the future. Thus, power is a relation; it is the way certain actions relate to other actions by constituting them to a greater or lesser degree, but never completely.

As a relation of actions upon other actions, power is not itself a strength that inheres in individual actors or that comes into being in collective ones "in the formation of a common or joint will through a communication directed toward consensual agreement."[3] Power is not a substance that "springs up between men when they act together and vanishes the moment they disperse," the human ability to act in concert.[4] Even though the condition of "acting together," demonstrating "power in numbers," may be a resource for the exercise of power, power is not a quality of action (e.g., power*ful* or power*less*) but *a kind of relation among actions* (and, in any case, the consent implied in acting together presupposes the prior formation of acting subjects by a power relation, as I demonstrate below).

Further, as a relation among actions, power "is the name that one attributes to a complex strategical situation in a particular society."[5] Power is not held but exists only in its exercise, as the acting of actions upon other actions. Power relations are therefore "intentional but nonsubjective"[6] in that the exercise of power is imbued with calculation—objectives, and methods for achieving them, which comprise a strategy—but there is no strateg*ist*, there is no one who invented them nor another instance that metaphysically explains them. The term "power" describes a strategic situation whose objective—the control of ac-

3. The quotation is from Jürgen Habermas, describing what he calls "Hannah Arendt's communications concept of power," as cited in Fred R. Dallmayr, *Polis and Praxis: Exercises in Contemporary Political Theory* (Cambridge, Mass.: MIT Press, 1984), 98.

4. Hannah Arendt, *The Human Condition* (Chicago: University of Chicago Press, 1958), 200. See also Hannah Arendt, "On Violence," in *Crises of the Republic* (New York: Harcourt Brace Jovanovich, 1972), 143.

5. Michel Foucault, *The History of Sexuality*, vol. 1, *An Introduction*, trans. Robert Hurley (New York: Pantheon Books, 1978), 93.

6. Ibid., 94.

tions by other actions—emerged, as in the case of sexuality, *historically*.

As I demonstrate in Chapters 3 and 4, using the historical specificity of how "coming out" "works," modern power is exercised in a *normalizing-disciplinary* mode.[7] This means, very schematically here, that although power is exercised over actions, in order to function it "manufactures" individuals who "will," whose bodies are at once the object upon as well as the instrument through which power is exercised; this is *discipline*. Norms, on the other hand, are the means by which such individualization can take place; they are at once a common standard of, as well as, here, a principle of comparability of, individuals. To say that power is *normalizing* denotes that its exercise relies upon standards on the basis of which actions (and the individuals who author them) are measured and guided as well as elicited. These norms themselves, however, come into existence through a society (or group) recognizing a principle of self-referentiality, a common denominator, by which everyone can shape, comparatively evaluate, and identify herself or himself as part of the society or group. Thus, a norm is purely relational: it is intrasocial and also provides the basis for all claims of individuality within the society. And the content of the norm that provides the basis for each acting upon the actions of others (i.e., discipline) will be *historical*—it derives from the strategic claims individuals have made and are making upon

7. This formulation of power is that of Michel Foucault in *Discipline and Punish: The Birth of the Prison*, trans. Alan Sheridan (New York: Pantheon Books, 1977), 170–228, and *The History of Sexuality*, 1:144.

the normative order of the social group or society. In sum, "disciplinary" describes the behavioral practices constituted through the exercise of power (e.g., "heterosexuality"), and "normalizing" refers to the standards or goals or outcomes (e.g., biological reproduction) toward which those behavioral practices are shaped up: a normalizing-disciplinary ordering of power that is historically specific to a particular society or group.

The norm is the society's or group's observation of itself; no one is the subject that established it, and it is created by the collectivity without being willed by anyone in particular. Norms are a society's relation to itself. Thus, the modern "average" or "normal" person is a fictional entity and also "society itself as it sees itself objectified in the mirror of probability and statistics. Once human nature loses its metaphysical status, individuals can be judged only with reference to the social, . . . to the average, . . . [which is] an instrument that makes it possible to understand a population with respect only to itself . . . [and for the latter] to make social judgments with respect to itself in a way that always reflects the current state of society and is based on normative, rather than prescriptive, evaluation."

A society or group will impose norms (through various techniques) as standards (how it defines the requirements of social life) on the basis of which performances of individuals will be evaluated and classified hierarchically. "Abnormality" is an individual's inability to perform adequately; but since the norm itself signifies not a natural quality or property of being but, rather, some aspect of the society's or group's relation to itself, the threshold between the normal and the abnormal is unstable. "Opposition to the particular [power] technique and the demands associated with it implies a will to modify the threshold for exclusion" (from the "normal" life of society) and debate over the boundary between normal and abnormal is meaningless without effort to alter the social conditions—what are conceived as the requirements of social life—that produced the boundary.[8] The lesbian and gay movement has tried to alter the social conditions that produce the boundary heterosexuality (normal) and homosexuality (abnormal) by opposing the principal techniques of power—domination and subjection—through which performance according to the norm, compulsory heterosexuality, is inculcated and people made governable.

These two principal techniques through which actions act upon other actions so that what has been designated power is exercised provide a focus for a politics of sexuality. *Domination* allows the actions of one to elicit and guide or command the actions of another with a high degree of certainty. This is because there is recourse to a structure of other actions that are brought to bear upon the actions over which power is being exercised and that have as their support culture, the law, social institutions, and economic processes.

In *subjection*, the second technique, actions elicit or shape other actions through which an author, sub-

8. This and the quotation in the preceding paragraph are from François Ewald, "Norms, Discipline, and the Law," *Representations* 30 (Spring 1990): 145–46, 158. My discussion of normalizing-disciplinary power is indebted to this essay, as well as to his "Power without an Exterior," in *Michel Foucault: Philosopher*, ed. Michael Armstrong (New York and London: Routledge, 1992), 169–75.

ject, or agent of those other actions is brought into being. It is a relation where actions control the behavior of an actor by establishing as an object of action the actor's identity and elaborating it as such. Subjection is a technique that creates an *identity*, by which I mean a procedure for having a relationship, in which power is exercised over one who is subjected by virtue of this identity. Unlike domination—a technique for exercising power in a relation between who obeys and whom must be obeyed—subjection involves obedience to oneself rather than to another (e.g., to one's conscience, one's "authenticity," one's identity). A relationship of power does exist, however, to the extent that the actions of *another* (or others) are controlling, to a greater or lesser extent, the actions that one performs in creating oneself as a subject capable of action. A subject or agent of action, therefore, does not exist a priori but is constructed within historically specific relations of power both as one over whom power is exercised and as one who is exercising power through a process of self-or autosubjection. For in order to subject another, one who is exercising power must form him-, her-, or itself into the kind of agent that can command obedience on the part of the other. This entails one's own subjection through other power relations that one then uses as resources in exercising power over others. One must, for example, subject oneself within the professional role of psychiatrist (dependent upon such matters as certification requirements, professional standards of conduct, legal norms regarding malpractice, etc., and medical definitions of mental illness) in order to be able to subject another as a mentally ill patient.[9]

Thus, power is exercised through a structure, network, or, more aptly, a *technology* that integrates the way individuals or groups are controlled by others (here, the technique of domination) and the extent to which this domination has access to the ways in which they constitute themselves as individuals or groups (the technique of subjection). Domination exists when the possibility of reciprocity of action upon the action of others is limited. One party to the relationship (whether an individual, a group, a class, a caste, etc.) exercises power, controls the other, in a more or less unilateral or asymmetrical way, and the possibility of changing those relations of power is almost nil at the individual level (it is a structure of domination that must be changed). To be sure, power is always exercised *indirectly*, not forcibly "on" bodies but "over" their actions, and "through" bodies using methods by which those actions are given agency. (Although

9. Thus, according to Hubert Dreyfus and Paul Rabinow, "power is exercised upon the dominant as well as on the dominated. [For example,] in order for the bourgeoisie to establish its position of class domination during the nineteenth century, it had to form itself as a class." But, although it did so intentionally, it did not do so subjectively; in the words of Michel Foucault: "One could say that the strategy of moralization (health campaigns, workers' housing, clinics, etc.) of the working class was that of the bourgeoisie. One could even say that it is this strategy which defined them as a class and enabled them to exercise their domination. But, to say that the bourgeoisie at the level of its ideology and its projects for economic reform, acting as a sort of real and yet fictive subject, invented and imposed by force this strategy of domination, that simply cannot be said" (Herbert Dreyfus and Paul Rabinow, *Michel Foucault: Beyond Structuralism and Hermeneutics* [Chicago: University of Chicago Press, 1982], 186; Foucault is cited therein).

power may operate on bodies, by doing so it does not force agents against or in spite of their will; rather, it shapes that will.) Not all exercise of power relies upon a structure of domination, but it does rely upon technologies or networks of power relations (the exercise of power is almost always not merely interpersonal); thus, politics always involves problematizing power relations *structurally*, that is, changing one set of power relations by changing another set of power relations. Thus, to change power relations between blacks and whites in the workplace, it has been necessary to change power relations in the educational system so that blacks can possess the expertise formerly monopolized by whites (and used as a resource to dominate them). Similarly, to abolish the legal restriction that prevented immigration of gays and lesbians into the United States, it was necessary for them to unite in a social movement and, at least as a first step, get the psychiatric profession to abolish the classification of homosexuality as a mental disorder, upon which the immigration statute had been based.

Domination, then, refers to that technique of a power relation where one individual or collectivity obeys another. Subjection refers (perhaps in that same relationship) to one's obedience to one's own conscience or sense of self, as individual or collective identity, where that conscience has been or is being shaped or modeled by another or others, and by virtue of which the actions of that other or others are exercising power in the relation. Techniques of domination and subjection are found throughout history. Modern subjection has as its object such individual human "needs" as health, happiness or adjustment to society, welfare (conceived as an adequate standard of living), protection against accidents, and so on. Through procedures like medical consultation, education, family policy, and employment, people are shaped—indeed, they are led to shape themselves, to consider themselves as having needs that require satisfaction.[10] At the same time, through the relation of subjection, information can be generated about such individual needs, by means of which individuals can be grouped into populations through which they can be known for regulation, their needs can be specified and satisfied, and, indeed, their potential as both individuals and populations can be conceptualized and then maximized. Subjection thus *individualizes* by creating a subjectivity in which one judges oneself (and accedes to judgment by others) according to the norm of the population to which one belongs—as has been suggested to one through the process of subjection. But individualizing through subjection is itself a technique through which the norms—the way a population, group, or society regulates itself—are inculcated in individuals that comprise that population. Therefore, the categories of domination and subjection describe techniques that can reinforce each other in how power is exercised in the everyday life of people—in the most minute details of their immediate relations with each other, in how those relations become intelli-

10. For a parallel analysis of the construction of needs, see Nancy Frazer, "Women, Welfare, and the Politics of Need Interpretation" and "Struggle over Needs: Outline of a Socialist-Feminist Critical Theory of Late Capitalist Political Culture," in *Unruly Practices: Power, Discourse, and Gender in Contemporary Social Theory* (Minneapolis: University of Minnesota Press, 1989), 144–60 and 161–87.

gible to them (as "healthy" or "perverse," for example), and in how they understand their own agency within those relations.

For example, early in the AIDS epidemic, when there were no competing hypotheses about AIDS etiology, and being diagnosed with antibodies to HIV (then HTLV-3) was conceived, by a univocal structure of medical expertise, as inevitably leading toward death, many of those so diagnosed took their own lives or submitted to life-threatening "treatments" since they had "nothing left to lose." However, within this structure of domination, such behavior consequent upon subjection could seem rational to those so subjected, and understandable to others who did not question the subjection. Similarly, one can conceive racial domination as a situation in which one group of people is able to exercise in a fairly consistent way (i.e., one that involves all members of that group) power over another group of people. Although it may or may not be rationalized through recourse to a biological inequality between the groups, what in fact distinguishes one group from the other on an interpersonal level are biological differences that have achieved their significance as a function of the relation of domination. The asymmetry in power exercised by individual members of the groups is reinforced by a variety of other power relations (such as the threat of legal or extralegal force, the power of educational institutions to certify competence, the capacity of the mass media to reflect and even shape opinion, etc.) that enable one group to maintain its dominance. This domination relies also upon the subjection of members of the dominated group. To the extent, for example, that they allow themselves to become the objects of knowledge of the dominant group, and then know and conduct themselves according to the subsequent norms established by the dominant group, they can participate in their own domination; or they can resist through the procedures by means of which such knowledge is produced within the structure of racial domination and thus undermine that structure.[11]

In the case of sexual behavior, domination privileges as normal (even though the tropes the society or group uses may be "natural," "healthy," etc.), and fosters, heterosexual sexual relations and disallows homosexual ones. The technique involves a variety of institutionalized means (educational, medical, religious, via mass media) through which power can be exercised to shape people's behavior according to the norm of reproductive (and gender) complementarity. This domination, referred to here as heterosexuality or, better, *heterosexism*, is complemented by procedures of subjection. They create, within the structure of heterosexist domination, individuals who understand themselves as "heterosexual" and, as such, can have access to the structure of domination to attain and maintain privilege and unequal social status relative to those not so subjected. Subjection also creates people who, to the extent that they do not perform in accordance with the norm of heterosexuality in their

---

11. For analysis along these lines, see also Michael Omi and Howard Winant, *Racial Formation in the United States*, 2nd ed. (New York and London: Routledge & Kegan Paul, 1994), and Kwame Anthony Appiah, *In My Father's House: Africa in the Philosophy of Culture* (New York and Oxford: Oxford University Press, 1992), especially chaps. 1 and 2.

choice of sexual partners, are shaped by the structure of heterosexist domination to understand themselves as social misfits. (This has been popularly called "self-hatred." It often involves an attempt by such an individual to "pass" as heterosexual—being "in the closet" except in that "parenthesis" within their lives, their "sex lives," which may also be infiltrated with the erotic roles of heterosexuality.) Just like the male-identified woman of feminist analysis, or the black skin/white mask phenomenon of colonized peoples,[12] there can be heterosexually identified lesbians and gays. Subjection creates people who are "heterosexual," psychically feeling superior and socially unequal to those who are "homosexual." These forms of subjection, of both "heterosexuals" and "homosexuals," may properly be termed *homophobia* (as they already have been by the movement): the subjective experience of normalizing-disciplinary power exercised through bodies, creating subjects of those bodies, who fear or are revulsed by homoeroticism. Heterosexist domination and homophobic subjection complement each other and, as I indicate, are socio-culturally and legally enforced through a technology of government, sexuality.[13]

---

12. Frantz Fanon, *Black Skin, White Masks* (New York: Grove Press, 1967), and Albert Memmi, *Dominated Man: Notes toward a Portrait* (New York: Orion Press, 1968). For a comparison of black, Jewish, and lesbian/gay oppression, see Barry D. Adam, *The Survival of Domination: Inferiorization and Everyday Life* (New York: Elsevier Inc., 1978).

13. The term "homophobia" was first used in George Weinberg, *Society and the Healthy Homosexual* (Garden City, N.Y.: Doubleday/Anchor Press, 1973). The utility of "homophobia" to describe the effects of heterosexism on an individual level has been criticized in Joseph H. Neilsen, "Heterosexism: Redefining Homophobia for the

To be sure, in an analysis of domination, power must be distinguished from violence. Violence acts upon a body as a relation of physical constraint tending toward complete determination. Power, as a relation among actions, presupposes two elements: that "the other" over whom power is exercised be recognized and maintained to the end as a person who acts; and that that other is free—faced with a power relationship, a range of responses and possible actions may be engaged in. Thus, power, while not excluding the use of violence as its ultimate resource and its limit, is distinct from violence; but when a power relation excludes the possibility of an acting other through complete determination by violence, it reaches its limit. Chaining someone up with the intent of simply allowing that person to die would not be a power relation but only a relation of physical constraint. However, to the extent that this action is a strategy to get the person to act in a certain way (say, to speak, when the person's ultimate recourse would be to resist speaking and die), power is exercised over someone capable of action, and it is intended to affect those actions.

Power, then, presupposes the possibility of action that is not completely determined, and a power relation is, strictly speaking, noncausal. More aptly, such

1990s," *Journal of Gay and Lesbian Psychotherapy* 1 (3) (1990): 21–35. The criticism is, schematically, that heterosexism is really a subphenomenon of sexism (unequal social roles played by biological males and females, i.e., gender) because gays, lesbians, and bisexuals do not conform to gender-role expectations. In the analysis that follows, I try to demonstrate how sexism and heterosexism are *discrete* forms of domination (with corresponding subjection), even though lesbians and gay men are affected by and often act to eliminate both of them.

a relation is agonistic—a reciprocal play of incitation and resistance, since, for it to be a power relation, the party over whom power is exercised must be *able* to act otherwise (even though it does not, to the extent power is successfully exercised). Freedom, on the other side, is therefore not an escape from all power relations ("nonpower") but, instead, the choice of action that can be constrained to a greater or lesser degree within power relations; and the extent of this choice is amenable to possible modification (the stuff of politics). Thus, while power and freedom are not opposites, physical constraint and violence are properly the opposites of power, since they ultimately fully determine the action of the one upon whom they are applied and set limits on the possibility for politics—changing power relations by means of the freedom that is their basis.[14]

Slavery is the threshold where power, through violence, can cease to be a power relation any longer and becomes one of pure determination. Orlando Patterson, in his book *Slavery and Social Death*, analyzes three aspects of slavery that are relevant to the analysis of power, violence, and lesbian and gay politics.[15] He describes slavery as one of the most extreme forms of domination. Slavery, first, was always considered as a substitute for death, usually violent death, and the relation was maintained through physical violence;

14. Thus, "Power and violence are opposites; where the one rules absolutely, the other is absent." However, "nothing is more common than the combination of violence and power, nothing less frequent than to find them in their pure and therefore extreme form" (Arendt, "On Violence," 155, 146).

15. Orlando Patterson, *Slavery and Social Death: A Comparative Study* (Cambridge, Mass.: Harvard University Press, 1982).

the slavemaster could at any time return the slave to its destiny. Second, to the extent that the slave was allowed to live, it lived in a state of what Patterson terms "natal alienation." The slave had at once no ties to ancestral blood family and its progeny belonged to the slavemaster; slavery was inheritable. As such, the slave was "socially dead"; it was not conceived as capable of enacting relationships that could, through contracting socially, establish itself as a social actor with a past and a future, which leads to another characteristic of slavery. Third, the slave had no self-determined social status; *any* status was determined by the master, on the master's terms. As such, to the extent it was given it was negative status—it was *dishonor* as compared with the honor accorded to the master that was subjectively experienced as self-hatred. Thus, the slave was not even considered an unequal "other"; indeed, it was not so much an "other" at all as a "thing," a "dis-other," a misfit. Patterson's definition therefore historicizes my analytical conceptualization of power's limit: violence tending toward pure determination; lack of otherness or personhood; and incapacity for action.

Without equating the brutality of slavery with the situation of lesbians and gays in our society, parallels can be drawn at the level of how the techniques of domination and subjection have changed historically. Male and female homosexuality is still punished with death in many parts of the world, and where it is not it is often punishable by imprisonment. To the extent lesbians and gays are allowed to live, the threat of violence is still an important resource for the exercise of power; the possibility of being gay-bashed or encountering another social reprisal short of violence is an important reason why gay men and lesbians do not show interpersonal affection in public the way heterosexuals do. While the role of outright violence cannot be dismissed, the cultural analogue of "social death" that lesbians and gays experience is significantly manifest in their rejection from families of birth, the society's unwillingness to allow them to marry and rear children, censorship of their production of artifacts that could transmit culture across generations, and inability to contract laterally for housing, employment, and essential services *as* lesbian or gay. Social death—institutionalized heterosexist domination—is reinforced, following Patterson's analysis, on a personal level through dishonor (homosexuality as abomination or abnormality) and subjection (the love that dares not speak its name) that results in lesbian and gay self-hatred. How this is different from slavery is in the way power has historically come to be exercised: instead of obedience to a master, this obedience is to oneself, but a self that is shaped through power exercised by formally equal (homophobic) subjects in everyday life, the subjection of self-hatred and negation of selfhood; instead of the direct diadic power that is exercised through the master-slave relation, power is now exercised *indirectly* through disciplinary practices (the educational canon, cultural media's non- or misrepresentation of homosexuality, codes of interpersonal comportment, spousal benefits—broadly conceived—that disallow gay relationships) by means of which behavioral norms constitute a structure of domination, heterosexism, and deter one's capacity to act *as* lesbian/gay—social death. This is in a cybernetic relationship with the procedures of subjection where homosexuality need not be directly and visibly "repressed" to the extent that, through individuals' self-regulation, it is invisible. However, where the discipline of remaining "in the closet" to enforce the norms of heterosexism breaks down, homophobic individuals (with or without recourse to institutional support) restore disciplinary power through force or violence. Given this seeming double bind, how is transformation possible?

Subjection, Lesbian/Gay Identity, and Agency

Subjection, as a technique through which power is exercised, therefore raises a fundamental problem—how to analyze the "self," "identity," or "individuality" as an element of social control (because of its being constituted within power relations) while acknowledging the existence of liberty or free agency (the condition of possibility for power to be exercised) in the context of subjection. If identity is socially constructed within a power relation, on what basis can action be free? A starting point in solving this seeming paradox is that we constitute ourselves, as agents who act, in relations with others. To be sure, we follow legal and moral codes, but what is more important for this analysis is the ethical domain: our relation with our self, what we call our identity (gender, sexual, racial, ethnic, etc.) and the conscience or self-knowledge that we use as a guide, and how it comes into being. Although such an ethical subjectivity, especially conscience, feels private and authentically "ours," it in fact gets formed through practices that are learned from the culture in which we live and that engage us in relations with others. Michel Foucault posited four components to, or moments of, working on oneself, in acting to constitute oneself as a distinct agent who acts in relation to others. That ethical self-constitution involves discrete *social* practices: (1) the ethical substance, or that part of ourselves we are working on when constituting ourselves as an agent in relation to others (e.g., our conscience, our sexual and affectional "feelings" with regard to erotic agency); (2) the mode of subjection, or how we use authoritative external sources to work upon ourselves—because of what we believe to be a rational norm of health (physical or psychological), because we are following the rule of a religious tradition, and so on; (3) the specific practices, techniques, or "ascesis" we use to give shape to ourselves, such as, for example, self-decipherment, as in psychoanalysis, participation in "consciousness-raising" groups or a regimen of abstinence or even deliberate "promiscuity" in erotic life; and (4) the kind of being to which we aspire in constituting ourselves, the telos of our conscience or ethics, be it historical immortality, personal liberation, or aesthetic appreciation by others, to name a few such possible goals.[16] Obviously, the individual does not just invent practices for constituting the self and employ them in solitude. They are suggested by or imposed upon us by the culture in which we live, they engage us in relations with others, and they are informed by the values and norms of our

16. Michel Foucault, *The History of Sexuality*, vol. 2, *The Use of Pleasure*, trans. Robert Hurley (New York: Pantheon Books, 1985), chap. 3 of the Introduction.

culture; indeed, they are, strictly speaking, the morality—or at least its codified elements—of a culture. Nevertheless, the different ways in which individuals create, elaborate, take care of, and change their own selves provide a perspective from which to analyze the existence of freedom as power's limit in any relationship, that is, ethics.

For example, the precise character of the ethical substance that becomes the center of a person's attention in self-constitution varies from culture to culture and over time. (As Foucault described it, the substance of Western sexual ethics changed historically from "aphrodisia" to "the flesh" to "sexuality," and, as I suggest, is perhaps now changing again.) Similarly, the mode of subjection, the way in which people in a society are encouraged to recognize norms, what rules they are to employ to work on their own ethical substance, allows for greater or lesser individual choice of what authorities to use. Feminism and Afrocentrism, for example, are deliberate and collective transformations of the mode of subjection of dominated categories of individuals. The specific techniques one uses to elaborate oneself may be a personal choice to "come out of the closet" within a specific social role such as one's occupation (which challenges homophobic subjection), or to remain in the closet (which accedes to it while elaborating oneself within a structure of heterosexist domination—for example, by "passing" as heterosexual). Even the kind of being aspired to by self-forming activity, while reinforced by the power of social valorization of individual behavior in any culture, is also an aspect of self-formation in which freedom is exercised in congruence with or divergence from dominant cultural values. (For example, a woman who values a career equally with raising a family differs from one who subordinates career to family, but the possibility of a career for a woman must exist for this to be the telos of her ethical self-constitution.)

Freedom, therefore, is not incompatible with the controlling power of subjection that, through external social categorization, can create an identity for an actor, thereby pressuring him or her to act within the category of the given identity. However, while power acts upon actions, to the extent that individuals have recourse to a variety of relationships through which they can constitute themselves as subjects of their actions they can act differently from what might be elicited or shaped through the exercise of normalizing-disciplinary power over their actions. Thus, for example, the possibility of the "liberated woman" or the "woman-identified woman" emerged as a result of women inventing new identities through "consciousness raising" and other new relationships with other women, rather than only or primarily through relationships with men (which had produced the "male-identified woman"). Such identities allowed them both to act differently interpersonally with men and to act collectively to change structures of male domination. Similarly, the political identity of "gay" was invented in opposition to the medically derived category of "homosexual" because of the self-affirmative relationships gay women and men were able to form among themselves (as distinct from having primary relationships with those who recognized them as social misfits, if an individual "came out" socially at all to nongays). It is for this reason—that freedom implies a variety of possible relationships within which the subject may constitute itself as an ethical agent of actions—that I argue for a *relational right*, for freedom of choice of and within one's relationships (rather than mere freedom of actions).[17]

To be sure, within a state of domination, the exercise of power has recourse to processes by which the individual (or group) acts on him-, her-, or itself. Inversely, the operations for constituting the self may be integrated into structures of domination so that the exercise of power need not merely coerce people, but rather combines processes through which the subject obeys others with processes through which that person constructs or modifies him- or herself. And here, the domination and subjection of lesbians and gays differs from forms of domination and subjection of other groups. Unlike oppression involving gender and race or ethnicity, where members of these groups have everyday social visibility (albeit as unequal to the dominant group), lesbians and gays can be socially invisible. The logic of lesbian and gay subjection leads to the preemption of agency constituting "the closet" (as gays and lesbians phrase it, "living a lie") and, in extremis, to suicide among lesbians and gays (the latter is particularly acute, because of their isolation from others, among lesbian and gay youth).[18]

---

17. See my discussion of the relational right in Chapter 4.

18. For example, "according to a 1989 study first commissioned and then squelched by the [U.S.] Department of Health and Human Services (HHS), gay youth are two to three times more likely to attempt suicide than heterosexual youth, and up to 30% of those teenagers who do commit suicide are gay or lesbian." Another study, published in *Pediatrics* in June 1991, reported that 30 percent of gay youth attempt suicide near the age of fifteen and that almost one-half of gay and les-

For lesbians and gays, the procedures of subjection that constitute the closet within the context of heterosexist domination result in preemption of selfhood as it is defined *through* agency—they are tolerated only to the extent they do not *act* homoerotically *socially* (as in slavery, they must be socially dead). And since power exercised through subjection elicits and shapes selfhood through regulating agency (again, power consists in actions upon actions), lesbian and gay "liberation" involves a *creation* of selfhood by reversing the very procedures through which one's (homoerotic) agency is preempted. The battleground then becomes the disciplinary practices through which one's actions receive normative recognition by others, which in turn effects the values—society's reflection upon itself through statistics, opinion samples, and so on—that render homosexuality invisible.

Thus, what happens to the institutions that "oppress" (by which I mean, do not foster, and indeed disallow, same-sex sexuality and its implications for the life course of individuals) is that their normative content is transformed. While, like participants in other civil rights movements, lesbians and gays want to be treated as equal citizens, their struggle, in en-

---

bian teens interviewed said they had attempted suicide more than once. The former study was denounced by a conservative congressman, William Dannemeyer, who asked HHS to disavow the report; in his view, "The last thing these individuals [gays and lesbians] need is a perception of accommodation from the Bush administration." Secretary of Health and Human Services Louis Sullivan responded by stating that, although youth suicide is an important issue, the views in the study "undermine the institution of the family"; no government action was taken on the report. See "Teen Suicide: The Government's Cover-up and America's Lost Children," *The Advocate*, no. 586 (September 24, 1991): 40–47.

gaging in hetero/homo inequality, is directed at and transforms, for example, the "normativity" of sexual relations—what relations "count" as sexual, their importance in individual lives and as a factor in social relations. In challenging their exclusion from the institutions of marriage, child-bearing and -rearing, as well as their own families of birth, lesbians and gays transform the norms defining kinship and biological reproduction, suggesting a redefinition of what love consists in, what kinds of affective relationships can be possible, and how these relations should be recognized socially. In embracing masculinity as a relation of equality among males, the social appearance via "coming out" of "masculine" gay men is a demand for equality, but it also transforms the cultural norms of manhood to the extent they are defined through sexuality as a complement to "the feminine"; it therefore transforms gender as such. This is not so much a revolution or a total transformation of society, as the reactionaries' threat of a "culture war" poses it. What is at stake, instead, is a challenge by a dominated group to those social norms (through the techniques of subjection by which they are enforced) that constitute its domination—and, in this case, whose logic tends toward *elimination through disallowance of the dominated group* (socialization toward "heterosexuality," closeted invisibility, and self-hatred; *social* death for lesbians/gays). To be sure, this is not necessarily the elimination of homosexuals or homosexuality directly (as in genocide or conversion therapy) as it is the regulation of *agency* so that one becomes as a ventriloquist's dummy to power that "disciplines" toward the normal; in this case, toward oblivion. "Gay" and "lesbian," therefore, denote the introduction of agonic agency into those relations of power exercised through sexual domination and subjection; as such, this is preeminently political.

Thus, as I set forth below, lesbian and gay politics is "identity politics" in the specific sense that it involves reversal, sometimes ironically, of procedures within our culture by which people are subjected and attributed an identity (through self-examination of one's thoughts, as suggested by cultural authorities, and by verbalizing these thoughts—making them socially visible—to such authorities, who then guide one in shaping oneself through continuous reexamination and reverbalization). It is through a reversal of these disciplinary procedures of subjection in which the self is at once invoked and then regulated that coming out's behavioral performance on behalf of a lesbian or gay identity challenges and transforms the norms constitutive of heterosexist domination. (This identity is dependent upon the existence of others who share that identity through a different mode of subjection as a source of authority.) In modernity, the "self" is produced through these procedures of subjection—self-examination and verbalization, giving oneself a socially visible identity—but the self is also an effect of one's agency within those power relations that can then transform them. "Coming out" is the way we talk, today, about agency that reverses the exercise of power operating through subjection, resulting in the constitution of selfhood. Coming out as gay or lesbian, creating oneself as an agent of one's actions in the context of power exercised through relations of sexuality is thus a preeminently political act of "empowerment"; it also links ethics to politics, as I shall demonstrate.

Sexuality has historically become central to how modern forms of power reach individual subjectivity and hence to how agency of behavior is created. Since sexuality seems private and "essentially" ours, it is a way, through subjection, that "self-" or "auto-regulation" takes place. While this procedure of social regulation operates on all members of society, for lesbians and gays it is crucial, since it is their sexual behavior that has historically come to be labeled sinful, unnatural, abnormal, and illegal, and come to be, through domination and subjection, rendered interpersonally and culturally invisible and subjectively understood as a personal deficit. Finally, this domination and subjection through *sexuality* is therefore a different phenomenon than that of gender and race or ethnicity; it is neither more nor less "oppressive," although some individuals will resist oppression on the basis of an identity derived from overlapping gender, racial, and sexual domination and subjection. However, what is at stake in lesbian and gay politics, derived from coming out—a politicization and ultimately a refusal of subjection based in domination—is an issue that members of all these groups share: a limit to power in ethics.

Domination and subjection are not the only techniques through which power can be exercised. Even dissolution of such historical forms of domination as racism, sexism, and heterosexism, while opening up new and perhaps more flexible relationships of power (limited by the freedom of ethical self-constitution), simultaneously opens up new possibilities for domination—understood here as the monopolization or hegemonization of power relations.[19] The exercise of power—people being able to determine the behavior of others—inheres in all social life; it exists to the extent that individuals, in their interpersonal relations, have recourse to other power relations (that may be derived from economic resources, cultural traditions, and so forth). But, for the political analysis of the exercise of power, domination and subjection are the most important of techniques, because they demarcate the limits of power's exercise. States of domination, taken to the extreme, would eliminate freedom—the precondition for the exercise of power (slavery or the imprisonment of one group by another would be examples of such an extreme state). Subjection also, taken to its extreme, limits power. Besides the social death resulting from domination, the invisibility of other lesbians and gay men for each other to perceive, as a condition for and combined with a subjective relation to oneself as a social monster (to the extent that it results in the suicide of the one so subjected), is power's limit too,

19. James Scott's definition of domination parallels my own and is suggestive for the situation of lesbians and gays. It includes: (1) institutionalized means of extracting labor, goods, or services from a subject population ("institutionalized" = "the closet"); (2) formal assumptions about superiority of dominant and inferiority of subordinate groups (heterosexism and homophobia); (3) status in domination is ascribed at birth, mobility is virtually nil, and subordinate groups are granted few if any civil/political rights (for "out" lesbians and gay men); (4) although institutionalized, it contains a strong element of arbitrary and capricious rule (e.g., gay-bashing, bigoted remarks), with personal terror suffusing the dominant/subordinate relationship (fear of exposure); and (5) within an extensive offstage social existence, the subordinate group develops a shared critique of power (geographic "gay ghettos," gay and lesbian culture and institutions). See James Scott, *Domination and the Arts of Resistance: Hidden Transcripts* (New Haven: Yale University Press, 1990), 21.

since there would be no subject over whom to exercise power. Death is power's limit; both slavery and the closet, as social death, are the threshold of that limit.

Political critique consists in analyzing how domination works both to constrain the kinds of relationships people can have with each other and to constrain who can exercise power in those relationships. It consists as well in analyzing how the possibility of action is itself constrained through individual and group subjection. But as African Americans, women, and now lesbians and gays have shown, what is crucial in reconceptualizing an existing set of relationships *as power relations* is the awareness oneself and the capacity to demonstrate to others that the definition of such relationships is a reason why the one who is exercising power over you does so. And it is this third aspect of power that leads to why lesbian and gay politics involves a politicization of "the truth." Lesbians and gays politicize their situation because of their erotic experience. In doing so they problematize, on the basis of their own experience, socially circulated ideas about sexuality since domination and subjection of them is able to occur largely *because* of such truth claims about sexuality.

Sexuality and Truth

Contrary to an old chestnut, the political relevance of truth is not that "knowledge is power." Rules for establishing what is true and false are not themselves power relations, nor does power directly produce knowledge, as in the Marxian theory of ideology and false consciousness. Rather, the extent to which a society values truth will imply the correlative existence of power relations in objectifying aspects of life about which to make rules distinguishing true and false, and the institutionalization both of those rules as knowledge and of people who, by virtue of knowing those rules can "tell the truth" (in our society these people are called "experts"). Further, the objectification of an aspect of human life as something about which the truth must be known means that some people will be able to exercise power over others. For example, people have been confined and subjected to psychosurgery for homoerotic behavior deemed a mental illness by experts, psychiatrists; children are taught what are the correct sexual behaviors and the dangers of the incorrect ones by teachers informed by knowledge about human sexuality; and in some jurisdictions, women may not refuse sexual relations with their husbands. All of these examples demonstrate that the truth about sexuality makes it possible for some people to exercise power over others that depends upon an objectification of certain human behaviors rather than others as "sexual" through rules distinguishing true from false that have been institutionalized as knowledge or expertise.

It is through this installation of sexual relations into a regime of truth that "sexuality" has been historically constructed as what I call a technology of government. This is the construction of a domain of human existence, sexuality, consisting in a body of knowledge about what sexuality is that informs a normative system of actions upon other actions—power—that constitutes those actions as sexual, and practices by which individuals—in the context of those power relations and using that knowledge by means of practical rules—construct themselves as sexual subjects. To be sure, sexual behavior need not be a matter for a discourse of true and false at all; it could merely be a question of physical sensations and pleasures according to personal taste—how people give themselves and each other bodily care. Nevertheless, today, as a consequence of the lesbian and gay political movement, sexual behavior is beginning to be conceptualized as a practice through which one constructs oneself as an *agent* of actions that can be appreciated by others according to criteria of how one, as agent, invents one's autonomy *through* sexual relations—a stylization of one's freedom—from which others can learn and adapt for constituting *them*selves. As I explain in later chapters, this involves the creation of a new ethic (doing so, for example, through participation in community institutions, with reference to other lesbians and gays as "role models," etc.) distinguishing this as a specific way of relating sexuality primarily to aesthetic claims to truth rather than to claims about human nature (albeit with claims for biological shaping of "orientation"—but *one* factor in sexual behavior).[20]

20. At issue is what role truth claims play in sexual behavior conceived as ethical self-constitution. Other approaches to sexuality and truth: Judith Butler, "Sexual Inversions, " in *Discourses of Sexuality: From Aristotle to AIDS*, ed. Domna C. Stanton (Ann Arbor: University of Michigan Press, 1992), 344–61; Elizabeth Grosz, "Refiguring Lesbian Desire," in *The Lesbian Postmodern*, ed. Laura Doan (New York: Columbia University Press, 1994), 67–84; Gilbert Herdt, "Representations of Homosexuality: An Essay on Cultural Ontology and Historical Comparison, Parts I and II," *Journal of the History of Sexuality* 1 (3 and 4) (1991); Simon LeVay, *The Sexual Brain* (Cambridge, Mass.: MIT Press, 1992); Richard Posner, *Sex and Reason* (Cambridge, Mass.: Harvard University Press, 1992); and Judith Roof, *A Lure of Knowledge: Lesbian Sexuality and Theory* (New York: Columbia University Press, 1991).

Lesbian and gay politics, then, has problematized not only the normative status of hetero/homosexuality and the instances of power exercised on the basis of this normativity as heterosexist domination and homophobic subjection but the entire installation of sexuality into a regime of truth and how, historically, it has become a technology of government—techniques through which people are governed and how they come to understand themselves and their own agency. To state this schematically within a historical perspective, through a sequence of changes—intellectual, social, and political—from the sixteenth through the nineteenth centuries, sexual practices that defined the sin and crime of sodomy were reobjectified. They were labeled a deviation of the sexual instinct by the emergent science of psychiatry, which institutionalized this knowledge as "homosexuality," a mental disorder. In turn this "disorder" could be diagnosed and treated (forcibly if necessary, but more efficiently through the patient's own willingness to be cured) by individual psychiatrists. These experts exercised considerable influence with regard to power exercised over people diagnosed with homosexuality (e.g., occupationally, within military service, legally, and through public mental health policy). Psychiatric expertise created a category of diseased people, homosexuals, whom psychiatrists tried to cure, at least in part, by getting the person so diagnosed to accept the category "being diseased" and to cooperate actively in the cure (i.e., to submit to the power exercised by virtue of psychiatric expertise). And even though the U.S. lesbian and gay movement successfully lobbied the American Psychiatric Association to remove homosexuality from its list of mental disorders in 1973, the relationship between sexuality and truth—how and why people's sexual behavior became a key to their intelligibility, the institutionalization both of knowledge about sexuality and of experts who know and tell the truth about people based upon their sexual behavior, and people who exercise power over other people *because* of the truth claims about sexuality—has been central to lesbian and gay politics. (This concern with truth on the part of lesbian and gay politics has included the truth about what "AIDS" is, whether lesbians and gays can make "true" families and parents, what specific erotic practices "truly mean" about one's personality and one's relationship with another, etc.)

This politics of truth of the lesbian and gay movement has been made possible, as I discuss in Chapters 3, 4, and 5, through (1) erotic practices that provide, on the body itself, a relation to oneself, subjectivity, that is an antidote to homophobic subjection in the context of heterosexist domination; (2) relations with others, ranging from friendship networks to institutions, which incubate and allow for the growth of shared values and thus the creation of different modes of subjection—sources of authority—than homophobic/heterosexist ones; and (3) a transformation in what sexuality is conceived to be, derived from making one's own sexual choices intelligible through claims different from the truth claims that have historically grounded sexuality. These claims are aesthetic—of personal taste—but also individually edified and are socially valorized with reference to truth, for example: to the logic of how to create oneself as an ethical agent of one's actions through gay or lesbian sexual and social relationships—the constitution of one's freedom—within the structure of heterosexist domination and homophobic subjection and the knowledge-by-example this yields for others on how to do so too; to the knowledge of sexual techniques and of medical risk factors; to the political understanding (to which coming out yields access) of one's situation within an order of power exercised through sexuality that contributes to an understanding of other power relations.

Thus, lesbian and gay politics reconfigures the relationship between sexuality and truth on the basis of how individuals construct themselves—the truth claims made by virtue of their constituting their own freedom through their sexual agency—and how others can learn from this to live fulfilling lives. This is the political significance of what has come to be called "lesbian and gay studies": discrediting the truth claims of heterosexism by producing statements derived from the new value created in the ways of living of lesbians and gay men and then institutionalizing *this* as educational curricula and through knowledge and expertise that can allow for the transformation of the disciplinary exercise of power—the social conditions underlying the boundary between the normal and the abnormal—so that normative change can occur and the life choices of lesbians and gay men included among the normal. (To reiterate: by "normal" I do not mean adaptation to heterosexist norms but the creation of different norms from what lesbians and gay men value—and their re-creation.) Indeed, if politics is about power, if truth is a qualification through which power can and must be exercised in this society, and if sexuality is one important way that the truth comes to be known about the people over whom power is to be exercised as well as how they come to know themselves and thereby become agents of their actions, then the shape of human reality at the present time—*how* to live—is at stake in lesbian and gay politics.

Politics and Technologies of Government

Politics involves problematizing how the ways individuals constitute themselves are linked with how their behavior is controlled by and controls others through a discourse of truth. The concept of a technology of government is an attempt to make this object of contemporary politics intelligible. Lesbian and gay politics, therefore, is concerned with how what we experience as sexuality has been historically constructed as such a technology of government.

Recall that power relations are "intentional and nonsubjective." Intentionality gives actions that act upon other actions their intelligibility. Actors who exercise power are usually quite clear about their objectives, and it is their articulated aims, their conflicting wills, and the fact that any strategical situation is imbued with calculation and explicit rationality that makes power relations decipherable. However, even though power relations are intentional, there is no overall coordination of them, no conspiracy, no Archimedean point (or corporate-state boardroom) from which an individual or collective subject presides over them—power relations are nonsubjective. Even "the state," whose contemporary role is to provide for some degree of coordination of and accountability for power relations according to a particular rationale, does not act as a coherent and calculating subject. This is not to say that there is not an overall direction or strategy to power relations, as I have suggested in the case of sexual domination and subjection. Power relations can constitute "systems" that have diverse resources and "do" things; but no organized group can be said to have subjectively invented them. I call these systems of power "technologies" to express how power works without a subject—such systems have come into being *historically*. Further, they are technologies of *government* because they involve the conscious intention of those actors who act within them (the term "government," how I direct behavior, my own and that of others, reflects this intentionality)—to act upon actions, self-shaping my own, in accordance with authoritative guidelines or authorities, as well as the actions of others.

While all social life involves normativity, collective standards of comparison and evaluation that rely upon the operation of power relations to a greater or lesser extent, normativity in modern times has increasingly become *government*: the bringing of domains of social existence into systems of power that act upon people's actions as well as through how they constitute themselves as subjects, and do so with explicit calculation according to a body of knowledge. Government is the point where structures of domination and techniques of subjection can complement each other, but can also be transformed. It is the point at which "the personal" and "the political" are linked. The personal—that is, ethics, one's relation to oneself or the constitution of oneself as an agent of one's own actions—exists both within a situation where one obeys another and within a situation of subjection where one obeys one's conscience as it has been shaped by external authorities. Government involves the extent to which one's actions accede to a power relation by virtue and by means of ethical self-constitution, or the extent to which they do not, and an explicit rationale for why they do not is formulated (which could then contribute toward politicization). On the other side, governing people always involves an attempt by the governor to determine the conduct of the governed (to exercise power) through processes by which the one who is governed constructs his or her own personal identity. As such, government entails a practice of the self that inheres in one's exercise of power over others, as well as that implicated, by virtue of subjection, which allows one to exercise power over another or others. Recall the psychiatrist who was formerly able to govern homosexuals as individual cases of a diseased population by virtue of her or his medical expertise as constructed through the technology of government that is "sexuality."

Government, then, is how individuals, constituting themselves as subjects of their actions (their ethical freedom), are constrained by power that is exercised over them. Government also informs how they will exercise power over others. It can be how one constitutes oneself as a teacher and governs one's students, how one constitutes oneself as a spouse and/or parent and governs one's family, how one constitutes oneself as a public official and governs the activity of the agency for which one is responsible. Each is the point at which ethical self-constitution is informed by power relations and informs one's own exercise of power, according to a set of rules or a body of practical knowledge. Thus, technologies of government, rather than primarily either the state (which is really a composite of and register of the behavioral outcomes and overall direction of technologies) or interpersonal power relations (which are components of them), are the focus of analysis in studying power and the object—the problem—for practical political action.

Michel Foucault, too, analyzed what he called the deployment (*dispositif*) of sexuality. In using the concept *dispositif* (which has been variously translated as "apparatus," "regime," and "deployment"), he was concerned with how power operates as a strategy without a strategist, as a social formation of "discourses, institutions, architectural forms, regulatory decisions, laws, administrative measures, scientific statements, philosophical, moral and philanthropic propositions"[21] that emerged historically. Sexuality coalesced from the eighteenth century, as I set forth in Chapter 2, as a technology of government that integrates heterosexist domination and homophobic subjection and programs what lesbian and gay thinkers have called "compulsory heterosexuality."[22] As such,

21. Michel Foucault, *Power/Knowledge: Selected Interviews and Other Writings*, ed. Colin Gordon (New York: Pantheon Books, 1980), 194. For an analysis of such regimes in terms of what they make visible, the enunciations to which they give rise, and how people act within them, see Gilles Deleuze, "What Is a Dispositif?" in Armstrong, *Michel Foucault*, 159–66.

22. The conceptualization was developed in Adrienne Rich, "Compulsory Heterosexuality and Lesbian Existence," *Signs: Journal of Women in Culture and Society* 5 (4) (Summer 1980): 631–60. Discussion of her formulation followed in Ann Ferguson, Jacquelyn N. Zita, and Kathryn Pyne Addelson, "On 'Compulsory Heterosexuality and

sexuality is a concept that describes personal experience, to be sure, but as it is mediated through various institutions by means of which norms are transmitted and through forms of knowledge and procedures of subjection by means of which that knowledge, as expertise, allows for the interpretation of that experience that then shapes behavioral outcomes. The outcomes of this mediation are less the repression of individual behavior than the production and regulation of individual subjectivity—individuality as such—by organizing the context within which individuals make choices among erotic activities, types of interpersonal relationships, and consequent life options.

However, in Foucault's later studies of and writings on the history of sexuality, he suggested that maybe he had stressed the operation of power too much.[23] Indeed, in his interviews about gay life, based upon this participation in it, he described sexuality as follows:

> Sexuality is a part of our behavior. It's a part of our world freedom. Sexuality is something that we ourselves create—it is our own creation, and much more than the discovery of a secret side of our desire. We have to understand that with our desires, through our desires, go new forms of relationships, new forms of love, new forms of cre-

Lesbian Existence': Defining the Issues," *Signs: Journal of Women in Culture and Society* 7 (1) (Autumn 1981): 158–99.

23. His change in methodological direction from power to the self is mentioned in "Technologies of the Self," in *Technologies of the Self: A Seminar with Michel Foucault*, ed. Luther H. Martin, Huck Gutman, and Patrick H. Hutton (Amherst: University of Massachusetts Press, 1988), 19.

> ation. Sex is not a fatality, it's a possibility for a creative life.[24]

In taking the inverse perspective to that of an apparatus (that is, the perspective of subjective agency within the technology of sexuality), Foucault indicated that it is possible for us to analyze how techniques of power suggest themselves to subjects, through which they form themselves as such, and also how these practices of subjection are double-edged. From this perspective, the self is not a simple reflex of anonymous apparatuses of power. It contributes at times to making the apparatus work and at other times to resisting and thereby transforming it. It is in this way that I analyze sexuality as a technology: it is a dimension of life through which we come to understand and participate in social relationships that always already involve power, and we act through the technology; but it is also a tool that we use to have relationships with each other and to constitute our own agency so that one's self *becomes*. Sexuality is at once individual and social: it is a historically constructed form of conceptualizing and organizing human life according to certain criteria that include bodily practices that may excite toward, but do not necessarily include, orgasm, types of relationships among individuals, and more or less systematic knowledge about these phenomena. Sexuality is a technology of government because it is at the intersection of how we come to be shaped and constrained by others and how we use our freedom to constitute ourselves as agents of our actions.

---

24. Michel Foucault, "An Interview: Sex, Power, and the Politics of Identity," ed. Bob Gallagher and Alexander Wilson, *The Advocate* no. 400 (August 7, 1984): 27.

I am not the first writer to address technologies of government. Rosi Braidotti, in her critique of female sexuality, and Teresa de Lauretis in her book *Technologies of Gender*, have contributed to the analysis of the politics of gender—the politicization of the technology, the structure of domination and procedures of subjection—that constitutes and reproduces relations of inequality between women and men. The studies by Daniel Defert and François Ewald on the historical emergence in Europe of the technology of insurance governing individual lifestyle and its relationship with collective social risk, and the successive politicizations of insurantial technology, exemplify the kinds of analyses that need to be done of sexuality, of which this work, like that of Gayle Rubin, is a beginning. Peter Miller and Nikolas Rose have also done studies of the technologies of government operating through such institutions as the military, the business organization, the school, and the family, by means of which both "the economy" and modern subjectivity are managed and, indeed, the "self" comes into being.[25] In the

25. Rosi Braidotti also uses the term "technology" in reference to sexuality, but in a manner different from mine, emphasizing primarily the productive capacities of power rather than the interaction between these and ethical self-creation, the interaction that is government. See Rosi Braidotti, *Patterns of Dissonance* (New York and London: Routledge, 1991), 76–97; Teresa de Lauretis, *Technologies of Gender* (Bloomington: Indiana University Press, 1987); Daniel Defert, "Popular Life and Insurance Technology," and François Ewald, "Insurance and Risk," in *The Foucault Effect: Studies in Governmentality*, ed. Graham Burchell, Colin Gordon, and Peter Miller (Chicago: University of Chicago Press, 1991), 211–33, 197–210; Nikolas Rose, *Governing the Soul: The Shaping of the Private Self* (New York and London: Routledge, 1990); Peter Miller and Nikolas Rose, "Governing Economic Life," *Economy and Society* 19 (1) (February 1990): 1–31; and Gayle Rubin, "Thinking Sex: Notes for a Radical Theory of the Politics of Sexuality," in *The Lesbian and Gay Studies Reader*, ed. Henry Abelove, Michele Aina Barale, and David Halperin (New York: Routledge, 1993), 3–44.

pages that follow, I analyze how the kinds of erotic relationships we can have with each other are invoked and then managed through sexuality as a technology of government and how lesbians and gay men, because of their particular historical and strategic position within this technology, have made sexuality a political issue that allows us to understand the limits of power in the freedom through which ethical agency is created.

Chapter 2

A Politics of Sexuality

Getting pleasure [out of sex] is not my particular agenda; getting equality is. If sexual pleasure is in the way, we need to think about it.

Catharine A. MacKinnon

In this chapter I analyze how sexuality has become historically constituted as a technology of government, and how it therefore forms the object for politicization—that is, how it becomes a political issue or concern. By "politics," again, I mean making some aspect of social life into the object of a collective movement, of power relations that might include laws and institutions, and of reflection about it, through writing and speaking, *as* political—a historical ontology of politics.

The argument is presented in four stages. First, I discuss the character of modern power as biopower. Then, within this historical context, I survey some of the political struggles around biopower in order to demonstrate how sexuality becomes a political issue. Third, I explicate sexuality as a technology of government. Last, I present a framework for the analysis of how lesbians and gay men problematize this technology of government—the lesbian and gay politics of sexuality. I employ this framework through the rest of the book in analyzing how lesbians and gay men problematize subjectivity derived from sexuality and form themselves into a movement challenging the regulation of sexuality. I also investigate how, in so doing, they redefine the significance and use of sexuality for contemporary individual and collective existence.

Power in Modernity: Biopower

In order to conceptualize sexuality as a technology of government and analyze how it becomes an object for politics, it is first necessary to trace sexuality's emergence through its historical condition of possibility, what Michel Foucault termed "biopower." Biopower developed through historical circumstances specific to the West and was articulated by texts about the art of government beginning in the sixteenth century. According to Foucault, government gradually came to mean the art of exercising power over people in their relations with things that mattered to the strength of the state. Such things included territory and the means it provided for subsistence, as well as climate and wealth; customs, habits, ways of doing and thinking; and people in "their relation to accidents and misfortunes which are famine, epidemics, death, etc."[1]

Foucault contextualized this transformation in the exercise of power historically in the development (beginning in the sixteenth century) of the "administrative apparatuses of great territorial monarchies (the emergence of governmental apparatuses),"[2] The emergence of a science of the state in statistics, and the creation of an instrument for both the exercise of power and the collection of knowledge about the individuals and populations over which power is exercised, the police. Police, at the time this instrument was being developed, meant "the specific techniques by which a government in the framework of the state was able to govern people as individuals significantly useful for the world,"[3] that is, to increase the strength of the state's forces from within. (The other side of the knowledge/power of police technology is a diplomatic-military one, exemplified in the search for a European balance of power through the various treatises called the Peace of Westphalia [1648], which attempted to guarantee and develop the "outward" forces of the state by a system of alliances and the organization of an armed machine.)[4] Foucault con-

---

1. Michel Foucault, "Governmentality," trans. Rosi Braidotti, *Ideology and Consciousness*, no. 6 (Autumn 1979): 11.
2. Ibid., 14.
3. Michel Foucault, "The Political Technology of Individuals," *Technologies of the Self: A Seminar with Michel Foucault*, ed. Luther H. Martin, Huck Gutman, and Patrick H. Hutton (Amherst: University of Massachusetts Press, 1988), 154.
4. Michel Foucault, "Foucault at the College de France I: A Course Summary," trans. and with an introduction by James Bernauer, *Philosophy and Social Criticism* 8(2) (Summer 1981): 240.

trasted this new conception of the exercise of power with an earlier one, emblematized by Machiavelli: "The aim of this new art of governing is precisely not to reinforce the power of the prince. Its aim is to reinforce the state itself."[5]

The biopower hypothesis is therefore that the old "juridical-sovereign" power of seizure (of things, bodies, time, ultimately of life itself) levied on subjects, which "culminated in the privilege to seize hold of life in order to suppress it,"[6] was gradually overshadowed (though not completely replaced) by the "administration of bodies and the calculated management of life" (140). The older repressive power

> has tended to be no longer the major form of power but merely one element among others, working to incite, reinforce, control, monitor, optimize, and organize the forces under it: a power bent on generating forces, making them grow, and ordering them, rather than one dedicated to impeding them, making them submit, or destroying them. (136)

Western humanity learned

> what it meant to be a living species in a living world, to have a body, conditions of existence, probabilities of life, an individual and collective welfare, forces that could be modified, and a space in which they could be distributed in an optimal manner. . . . Power would no longer be dealing simply with legal subjects over whom the ultimate dominion was death, but with living be-

5. Foucault, "Political Technology of Individuals," 150.
6. Michel Foucault, *The History of Sexuality*, vol. 1, *An Introduction*, trans. Robert Hurley (New York: Pantheon Books, 1978), 136.

> ings, and the mastery it would be able to exercise would have to be applied at the level of life itself. (142–43)

Power thus became "situated and exercised at the level of life, the species, the race, and the large-scale phenomena of population" (137).

More specifically, biopower, power over life, came to be exercised across two axes. Statistics developed as a scientific knowledge of those things that were factors in a state's power and subsequently revealed the existence of the *population*, with phenomena that are specific to it and that become the object of government. Thus, one axis of the exercise of biopower became focused on regulatory control over aggregates of people, "populations," by means of variables of the life process, whether territorial, cultural, or biological, through which they were able to be identifiable as distinct populations and regulated as such. Population became the object of government—particularly a population's *welfare*, the characteristics that are intrinsic to its viability, such as its wealth, its health, and its safety. Power is exercised through interventions into and regulatory control over factors that are imminent to the population (life expectancy, diseases, reproduction, cycles of scarcity, etc.), but not necessarily with the full awareness of the individual people comprising the population (such as the stimulation of birth rates or in directing the flow of population into certain areas or activities—creating and regulating a labor force, etc.). Foucault called this axis of biopower a *biopolitics of the population*.[7]

7. Foucault, "Governmentality," 18, and *History of Sexuality*, 1:139.

The other axis across which biopower came to be exercised concerns individuals less as juridical subjects (by virtue of their legal status defined by, say, kinship) than as living, working, or trading beings. It became a concern to the extent that individuals could introduce a change, positive or negative, in the welfare of the population. This axis centers on "the body as a machine: its disciplining, the optimization of its capabilities, the extortion of its forces, the parallel increase of its usefulness and its docility, its integration into systems of efficient and economic controls, all this . . . ensured by the procedures of power that [may be] characterized [as] . . . an *anatomo-politics of the human body*." These two axes of biopower, an anatomo-politics of the human body and a biopolitics of the population, became the characteristically modern form of power, respectively: "anatomical and biological, individualizing and specifying, directed toward the performances of the body with attention to the processes of life . . . whose highest function was perhaps no longer to kill, but to invest life through and through."[8]

Finally, those same sixteenth-century treatises on the art of the governing "of children, of souls, of communities, of families, of the sick" made it possible to conceive of government more broadly than as merely the action of the prince to reinforce his power. The tacticians of modern *raison d'état*, concerned as they were with the state's ends "freed from a larger ethical order and from the fate of particular princes," put into practice a political rationality that "no longer sought

8. Foucault, *The History of Sexuality*, 1:139 (emphasis in original).

to achieve the good life nor merely to aid the prince, but to increase the scope of power for its own sake by bringing the bodies of the state's subjects under tighter and tighter discipline."[9] This made it possible for the state, and for the governmental regimes more or less authorized on its behalf, to exercise a positive and permanent intervention in the lives of citizens. In so doing, they governed an individual's subjectivity, as well as intersubjectivity in relations with others (to the extent they may have had a bearing on the programs of government), by affecting the possible choices through which an individual constructs a meaningful life for her- or himself, what later came to be called a "lifestyle."[10]

Thus, in one of Foucault's most provocative formulations, "the ancient right to *take* life or *let* live was replaced by a power to *foster* life or *disallow* it to the point of death."[11] Modern power over life, biopower, is exercised over individual bodies and effects their integration into systems of economic and social control. It is exercised, as well, over populations, administering the conditions that cause variations in propaga-

---

9. Hubert Dreyfus and Paul Rabinow, *Michel Foucault: Beyond Structuralism and Hermeneutics* (Chicago: University of Chicago Press, 1982), 137.

10. The analysis of how this is operationalized through, for example, individual psychological or vocational counseling and occupational-rapport groups, as well as through couples' and family therapy, would take the discussion too far afield. For a comprehensive examination of governing people through how each individual constructs a lifestyle, see Nikolas Rose, *Governing the Soul: The Shaping of the Private Self* (London and New York: Routledge, 1990), chap. 16. I return to individuals' lifestyles as an object for government when I discuss the "gay lifestyle" in the context of AIDS etiology and epidemiology and of the creation of a distinctive lesbian and gay ethos.

11. Foucault, *The History of Sexuality*, 1:138 (emphasis in original).

tion, birth rate, longevity, mortality, and level of health, for example. Sexuality is at the intersection of these two sets of processes. Indeed, it is a point of access of power through *disciplining individuals* (e.g., education about safe-sex techniques, sexual-dysfunction therapies, counseling the role of sex in everyday life activity) and through *regulating populations* (e.g., the development and dissemination of birth-control technologies, defining "family," monitoring and fostering them through casework and child welfare policies, testing for sexually transmitted diseases based upon population characteristics, and strategies for "culturally sensitive" public health intervention).[12]

Sexuality, as a site at which power is exercised, involves recognizing oneself as a sexual subject in the context of an administrative concern for the welfare of society. This means that, through various socializing agencies, such as sex education, therapy, entertainments, one comes to think of oneself as having sexual desires that need expression, either alone or in relations with others. One comes to believe that such "self-expression" is subject to certain management procedures on behalf of one's own self-actualization, on behalf of mutually satisfying sexual relationships with others, and on behalf of the welfare of the population. This management is accomplished through the mediation of physicians, therapists, social workers, educators, and others whose expertise comes from forms of knowledge about both the welfare of the pop-

---

12. Historical detail supporting this thesis may be found in Jeffrey Weeks, *Sex, Politics, and Society: The Regulation of Sexuality since 1800* (London: Longman, 1981), particularly chap. 7.

ulation and the happiness (or psychological adjustment) of each individual. Sexuality, therefore, is a principal point of access to individual subjectivity for the exercise of power in the modern age.

As the practice of modern government came to center upon population as its object, sexual conduct became important as one characteristic of the individual constituents of a population that lent itself to study and intervention. On the one hand, it was important for the state to know how its citizens were conducting their sexual relations, for this could affect the health, reproduction and future prosperity, eugenics, and security of the population. On the other hand, individuals had to be able to control the use of their own "sexuality," which they discovered by examining their consciousness and by verbalizing their thoughts to others who would interpret them so that the individual could know (and effect changes on) him- or herself. Thus, a whole domain for the exercise of power developed through sexuality, ranging from state fiscal measures and the waging of state campaigns, to moral and religious exhortations, to procedures by which individuals produce themselves in understanding and directing their own sexuality.

Sexuality Becomes a Political Issue

Sexuality emerged historically as a rationale for and as a grid of intelligibility through which we understand, and indeed enact our relationships with each other. As such, sexuality involved the historical development of modes of knowledge that define what counts as sexual, ensembles of norms and laws, derived in part from tradition and in part invented, that regulate our relationships with each other through our sexuality, and procedures through which each of us can recognize ourselves as sexual subjects—as subjects "with a sexuality" and as agents who engage in sexual activities and make sexual choices.

Beginning in the eighteenth century, the governmental concern with and construction of sexuality focused upon four general areas.

First, sex, although defined dimorphically and possessed by both women and men, takes the form of a *lack* in woman. It is defined for her wholly by the reproductive function, which constantly agitates her for her completion by a man, who possesses the plenitude she lacks. This female body was then treated as an aspect of the body politic, whose fecundity the state had to regulate. The body was finally metaphorized in relation to the space of the home and childrearing duties within it to construct the biologically—and, through socialization, psychologically—destined Mother. Foucault traced here women's "hysterization," no doubt in the context of a patriarchal social order.

In the second area of concern, sex was defined as a latency that, if allowed manifest and improperly regulated expression in those "preliminary sexual beings," children, would pose grave dangers for civilization when they became frigid, impotent, deviant, or otherwise maladjusted adults. Experts had to advise the family. Thus, from the perspective of biopower, the campaign against childhood masturbation can be seen, in eighteenth- and nineteenth-century bourgeois families, as constructing a private sphere where parents would take responsibility for their children (which formerly had been delegated to others), while the family itself would serve public-health functions (by means of procedures of subjection—"family medicine" for the bourgeoisie, authoritarian medico-hygienic philanthropic assistance for the poor).

Third, the political socialization of procreation, where social and economic measures were deployed to make couples responsible (in terms of the needs of the population for greater or fewer births), was founded upon the representation of sex as an insatiable appetite of genital pleasure that had to be either checked or channeled by a socially administered reality principle.

Finally, a sexual "instinct" was posited, predicated upon biological functioning that gave sex a teleological meaning. On this basis, pathology or anomaly could be diagnosed and treated through techniques to correct the deviation or, if incorrigible, protect the population from the anomaly.[13]

As a result, four privileged objects of knowledge emerged, with corresponding forms of surveillance, treatment and regulation (medical, psychiatric, and, less often, legal), and procedures through which individuals could recognize themselves as belonging to one of the problematical categories and participate in their own government: the hysterical woman and mother, the maladjusted child, the careless couple, and the perverted adult. In this fourfold governmental concern that creates modern sexuality, we can recognize the principal themes of the Freudian discourse

13. Foucault, *The History of Sexuality*, 1:104–5.

on sexuality: (1) female sexuality, penis envy, and the vaginal orgasm dependent upon the presence of a phallus; (2) the Oedipus complex; (3) the tension between the pleasure principle and the reality principle; and (4) the theory of the perversions as deriving from an individual's historical maladaptation and/or biological inadequacy.

In these four areas of governmental concern through sexuality we can also, genealogically, recognize how a politics of, a politicization or calling into question of, biopower exercised through sexuality has emerged in our time.

For example, in the first concern, we can recognize the feminist problematization of the subjection implicit in the psychoanalytic theory of female sexuality and of domination by institutionalized gender roles that support it. We can recognize the struggle for transformation, mediated by "consciousness raising," among other techniques, of the procedures through which feminine subjection takes place—education, communications media, the workplace, and even the gendering of the methodology and scope of scientific research.

Another contemporary mutation of the hysterization of women's bodies is the development of new reproductive technologies. An anatomo-politics of the body, in the service of a biopolitics of the population, constructs the human body as a socioeconomic resource, whether for labor, reproduction, mothering, or sexual pleasure; restrictions on abortion are an obvious governing of this "resource," but so, too, are new reproductive technologies. A feminist politics of sexuality tends to view new reproductive technologies within the context of patriarchal domination, seeing them as reinforcing it through the creation of new forms of subjection. According to one writer, Jana Sawicki:

> New reproductive technologies clearly fit the model of disciplinary power. They involve sophisticated techniques of surveillance and examination (for instance, ultrasound, fetal monitors, amniocentesis, antenatal testing procedures) that make both female bodies and fetuses visible to anonymous agents in ways that facilitate the creation of new objects and subjects of medical as well as legal and state intervention. Among the individuals created by these new technologies are infertile, surrogate and genetically impaired mothers, mothers whose bodies are not fit for pregnancy (either biologically or socially), mothers who are psychologically unfit for fertility treatments, mothers whose wombs are hostile environments to fetuses, mothers who are deemed "negligent" for not choosing to undergo tests, abort genetically "deficient" fetuses, or consent to caesarian sections. As these medical disciplines isolate specific types of abnormality or deviancy, they construct new norms of healthy and responsible motherhood. Additionally, insofar as the new technologies locate the problem of infertility within individuals, they deflect attention and energy that could be used to address the environmental causes of infertility. Hence, they tend to depoliticize infertility.[14]

She goes on to say that most women perceive these technologies as *enabling*, and that "by producing new

---

14. Jana Sawicki, *Disciplining Foucault: Feminism, Power, and the Body* (New York: Routledge, 1991), 83–84.

norms of motherhood, by attaching women to their identities as mothers, and by offering women specific kinds of solutions to the problems they face" such technologies continue the subjection of women in an overdetermined and continuously redetermined body (85). The feminist politics of sexuality, however, arguing from a right to privacy as control over one's body, uses the new procedures for subjection that these technologies present as an instrument to resist public appropriation of women's bodies. Such feminist politics also resists making motherhood a destiny of all women, or even of women at all, through support groups based upon these new "identities," thereby countering both subjection and decision-making practices that allow domination to coalesce. Feminist opposition to using the biopolitical imperative of, say, quality control of fetuses, which privileges some based upon their class or racial-ethnic origins, leads to a generalized demand for adequate and participatory prenatal health care for all similarly situated individuals.

But, to return to a feminist politics of sexuality per se, the discontinuities between the reproductive body, the gendered body shaped within heterosexuality by male domination, and the erotic body that lesbians invent is only now beginning to be elaborated fully. The lesbian discontinuity can be employed as a critique of the feminist politics of heterosexuality that further advances the feminist goal of women's erotic autonomy (see works by Butler, by Califia, by Grosz, and by Nestle cited throughout this book).

In the second area of governmental concern through sexuality, the eighteenth- and nineteenth-century construction of the sexualized family and childhood sexuality, we can recognize the source of gender-role socialization and its problematization. Freud theorized this by saying that women fantasized—when, in reality, they often actually experienced—incest, thus making it possible to justify gender-role socialization. His theory of homosexuality as arrested development in the progression from infantile polymorphous perversity to mature adult heterosexuality located the etiology of sexual orientation in the family (albeit with a caveat about possible determining biological factors). This theory of a sexualized Oedipal family provides a springboard for political programs for the elimination of homosexuality, as well as a justification both for its abnormality and for the hypostatized pathological consequences of lesbian and gay parenting.[15] We can also recognize the most "sensitive" governmental issues: When does parental or custodial affection become sexual and therefore constitute abuse? When can consent to sex be said to be given? (We shall recognize later, in the historical mutation from kinship to sexuality as a technology of government, the more contemporaneous sexualization of institutionalized power relations beyond the

15. One such program for its elimination based upon political suppression and socialization of the young is in William Dannemeyer, *Shadow in the Land: Homosexuality in America* (San Francisco: Ignatius Press, 1989). For an overview of the shortcomings of conversion therapy, see A. Damien Martin, "The Emperor's New Clothes: Modern Attempts to Change Sexual Orientation," in *Innovations in Psychotherapy with Homosexuals*, ed. Emery S. Hetrick and Terry S. Stein (Washington: American Psychiatric Association Press, 1984), 24–57. Recently, sociobiologists have joined the dispute with evidence that homosexuality is innate; see Natalie Angier, "Researchers Find a Second Anatomical Idiosyncrasy in Brains of Homosexual Men," *New York Times*, August 1, 1992, 7.

family, such as those between teacher and student, worker and supervisor, doctor and patient.) We can recognize here, also, the possibility for desubjectification by victims. Having retrospectively understood situations as abusive, they attempt both to change structures of domination (for instance, those of family "privacy," of the potential for workplace retaliation, of doctor-patient confidentiality) that allow the patterns of behavior to continue and to provide support networks for present and past victims of such abuses of power. Children's sexuality, finally, came to be monitored not only to ensure "normal" development but to create at the earliest age and then shape a self-consciousness (and thereby corresponding subjection) of one's own sexuality.

A third, and obvious, domain of government through sexuality that concerns procreative behavior can be seen in the political struggles over a woman's prerogative to terminate a pregnancy in the context of her body's having become a socioeconomic resource. Distinct from the possibilities for both eugenic and pronatalist or "limits to growth" governmental population policies, biopower has made the concept of life a *historical* event. A clinical blurring of the distinction between life and death has overshadowed (if not replaced) the principle of the absolute sanctity of life with that of the quality of life. Consequently, medical decision making and social policy take into account not only the quality of life of the mother and her health (more broadly conceived as psychological and socioeconomic welfare) but also what quality of future life can be expected for a fetus. In this sense, biopower tends to frame abortion as an issue of health and safety rather than as one of morality. Abortion is disallowing the future potential of life (as distinct from fostering the development of this potential). However, unlike the antiabortion movement, which would limit abortion to a decision made solely by a medical expert or a judge, the pro-choice movement's conditions of what counts as a rational argument derive from a tacit recognition of the context of biopower. Its argument expands the dimensions and pluralizes the sites of moral judgment in terms of social class and in terms of allowing women and others formerly disempowered to be coparticipants in what has historically been a hegemonically organized (by males, by experts—legal or ecclesiastical authorities) decision-making process.[16]

Further politicization of the procreative couple, primarily by lesbians and single women demanding access to infertility technology, uses new reproductive technologies to pull the rug out from under the anatomical and physiological grounding for reproduction. For example, what has been called the "lesbian baby boom" (indeed, single parenting by both gays and nongays), as well as surrogacy practices, call into question whether procreation need involve a couple at all. What is at stake here, ultimately, is a politics of sexuality that allows for reproduction without sexuality (in an interesting completion of the modern project to have sexuality without reproduction) and the vision of personal and relational fulfillment beyond the re-

16. My analysis is informed by Jeffrey Minson, *Genealogies of Morals: Nietzsche, Foucault, Donzelot, and the Eccentricity of Ethics* (New York: St. Martin's Press, 1985), chap. 8.

productive and gender complementarily of the heterosexual couple.[17] A contemporary politics of sexuality, therefore, questions state support for the procreative heterosexual couple as the sole or even the privileged definition of a family.

Fourth, and finally, the government through sexuality that constructs a "normal," instinct-based sexuality and that treats deviations from it with corrective therapies or isolation is challenged on behalf of all those means of sexual expression that are not genitally centered and are not reproductive. Obviously, the contemporary lesbian and gay movement is central to a politicization of "compulsory heterosexuality," but what is more interesting about this politicization is its limitations. There was a historical mutation from governmental concern with homosexual *acts* to a concern with the lesbian and gay *person*. Indeed, it was the refusal of the category "homosexuality"—via the positing, first, of "the homosexual" as deserving of society's toleration, and, more recently, the self-naming of a lesbian and gay culturally derived identity—that paved the way for depathologization, for debunking in the order of knowledge of homosexuality as arrested development and biological inadequacy and for its social acceptance as a "sexual orientation."[18]

17. This is the centerpiece of Roger Scruton's argument against homosexuality—that, by violating reproductive complementarity, it threatens the possibility of (albeit teleologically defined) other-directed love and is therefore an obscenity. Roger Scruton, *Sexual Desire: A Moral Philosophy of the Erotic* (New York: Free Press, 1986), 305–11.

18. For historical and theoretical perspectives, see Richard Isay, *Being Homosexual: Gay Men and Their Development* (New York: Avon Books, 1990); Kenneth Lewes, *The Psychoanalytic Theory of Male Homosexuality* (New York: Simon & Schuster, 1988), and George Weinberg, *Society and the Healthy Homosexual* (Garden City, N.Y.: Doubleday/Anchor Press, 1973).

This historical and political development exemplifies what Michel Foucault termed the mutation from a "juridico-discursive" coding of power and of subjects over whom power was exercised (exercised *through* law, in a negative or repressive way, over individuals by virtue of their specific, forbidden actions) to a "normalizing-disciplinary" exercise of power geared toward the production of subjects with good habits (i.e., those that will be socially useful)—the very historical mutation that sexuality as a technology of government accomplishes. Thus, from the point of view of government, and corresponding to criticism from within the rubric of biopower by the lesbian and gay movement, there is no longer homosexual*ity*-as-illness, there are simply homosex*uals*. From the point of view of biopolitics, such persons need to be integrated as productive members of society, defined as subpopulation by virtue of their sexual practices, and regulated as such (pedagogically, medically, economically). From the point of view of anatomo-politics, homosexuals are supposed to recognize their sexual "orientation" as gay or lesbian and establish "healthy" relationships with others. (As long as participants practice safer sex, the nature of their activities does not matter, even if they encompass so-called peripheral sexualities that are nongenital or nonreproductive, such as masturbation, sadomasochism [S/M], fetishism, etc.) Does this kind of normalizing specification of homosexuals and their regulation as a population mean that the government through sexuality inaugurated in the nineteenth century, and the subsequent politics of sexuality begun by the gay (and, later, lesbian and gay) movement, has been completed and "lesbian and gay liberation" achieved?[19]

Sexuality: A Technology of Government

Foucault suggested that what we call "sexuality" emerged through the anatomo- and biopolitical governance of those "four strategic unities"—women's bodies, the maturation of children, the reproductive couple, and the distinction between normal and abnormal sexual behavior through the positing of its source in a natural instinct. Together, these unities constitute what has been termed "compulsory heterosexuality" by feminist and lesbian-feminist thinkers. Heterosexuality is a social organization of power, what I have called a technology of government, that enforces gender inequality between biological males and females. It does so intrapsychically (*pace* Catharine MacKinnon) through heterosexual desire, and interpersonally and institutionally (*pace* Adrienne Rich and others) through marriage as necessary for women to survive economically and support children, through the negative consequences women who are not involved heterosexually and their children would suffer

19. To be sure, even the lesbian and gay movement has historically had great difficulty incorporating the diversity of sexual expression within its ranks. This is especially true of S/M, role-playing, bisexuality, transgendered individuals, fetishism, nonmonogamous partnering, "public" sex within institutions designed for this purpose, and the use of erotica. These have gradually come to be accepted as part of a pluralistic movement for "sexual freedom," although this concept is still a contested one within the movement, particularly among lesbian feminists. The result, however, has been to undermine the very notion of "peripheral sexualities," which was designed to negatively label nongenital and nonreproductive erotic expression.

from stigmatization as "abnormal," and through cultural representations that offer heterosexuality as exciting and the only viable option for women.[20] (Alternatives, especially lesbian ones, are either not represented or are disguised through congruence with the heterosexual norm.) Further, according to these theorists, it is *compulsory* heterosexuality because, under such conditions, women cannot be assumed to consent to heterosexuality (it is coerced consent at best), and many cultural practices actually enforce it in a repressive way (rather than only in a productive way fostering heterosexuality). Such cultural practices include criminalization of lesbian sexuality, rape (including marital rape and abuse), and "feminine" dress codes and sexual harassment on the job, among others. "Compulsory heterosexuality" was a term invented by feminists to explain how gender inequality is institutionalized and perpetuated; it was not invented primarily to explain homosexual oppression. To what extent does this conceptualization of sexuality explain lesbian and gay domination and subjection as such? How does compulsory heterosexuality, as a structure of power that includes repression, function in relation to the production and regulation of the self through sexuality?

---

20. Catharine A. MacKinnon, *Toward a Feminist Theory of the State* (Cambridge, Mass.: Harvard University Press, 1989), chap. 7; Adrienne Rich, "Compulsory Heterosexuality and Lesbian Existence," *Signs: A Journal of Women in Culture and Society* 5(4) (Summer 1980): 631–60; and Ann Ferguson, Jacquelyn N. Zita, and Kathryn Pyne Addelson, "On 'Compulsory Heterosexuality and Lesbian Existence': Defining the Issues," *Signs: Journal of Women in Culture and Society* 7(1) (Autumn 1981):158–99. A similar line of argument can be found throughout the various essays collected in Monique Wittig, *The Straight Mind and Other Essays* (Boston: Beacon Press, 1992).

The emergence of the concept of sexuality in the nineteenth century, as Arnold Davidson has documented,[21] corresponded to the historical emergence of specific types of normativity, correlated with forms of knowledge and procedures through which individuals come to know themselves that exist today. First, the emergence of sexuality consists in the gradual superimposition upon and supplanting of relations based upon biological kinship with relations of affinity derived from erotic practices and relations. As such, the circulation of sexual partners has less to do with marriage, the fixing and development of kinship ties, and the transmission of names and possessions than with the "self-realization" of—indeed, the intelligibility of selfhood to—the individual. This corresponds to the ascendancy of biopower, in that governmental regulation based upon kinship (derived ultimately from the ancien régime model of sovereignty and the right to rule because of blood line) is replaced (corresponding to the rise of the bourgeoisie) by multifaceted applications of power. This is achieved by means of detailed specification of bodies as producers and consumers and an increasingly comprehensive regulation of the populations that they comprise.

Second, sexuality is itself able to become an experience through the constitution of a field of knowledge drawn from the accounts of individuals. These accounts are collected by those who could interpret them with a view toward the body's intrinsic properties and laws, as well as variables of the population(s)

21. Arnold I. Davidson, "Sex and the Emergence of Sexuality," *Critical Inquiry* 14 (Autumn 1987): 16–48 (esp. 17–23).

of which the body may be a constituent element. Since the data involved in these investigations are proximate to anatomy, biological reproduction, and physiology, this field of knowledge that constitutes sexuality, to the extent that it is constructed by analogy with them, gains quasi-scientific status. Research into sexuality does not take as its object merely the reconstruction of the sexual act, its "what" and "how." Through personal histories, questionnaires, physical examination, and both recollection of conscious and interpretation of unconscious motivation, it translates these into scientifically acceptable observation and produces knowledge of individual bodies and of the life process. This yields access for biopower as an anatomo-politics of the human body and a biopolitics of the population. Sexuality can thus be conceived as a natural process (as affected by other ailments, but also with its own specific instincts, disorders, and their etiologies) and as susceptible to pathology and normality, thus calling for therapeutic interventions by medical and other specialists who could diagnose and cure or "normalize" any pathology.

Thus, the technology of sexuality consists in a construction of truth about the individual subjects and populations and expertise about and therapeutic techniques upon that level of human relations called "sexuality," as well as, third, procedures through which individuals can know *themselves* as subjects *with* a sexuality amenable to regulation. These procedures of subjection crystallize around the sexed body as bearer of a fundamental principle of identity. Sexuality is the procedure by which the *biological* (biological functions, anatomical elements, perhaps genetic predisposition, physical sensation) is united with the *historical* (gender, but also how sensations can count as pleasure) into an artificial unity that serves as a principle of intelligibility for selfhood. Being a subject with (a) sexuality is a procedure we use to make ourselves intelligible to ourselves, as well as a procedure (as sexual and gender identity) for having relations with others.

Sexuality, in sum, is a technology consisting of procedures through which individuals can know themselves, a system of knowledge, and types of normativity regulating individuals' relations with each other. Through this technology, the self is simultaneously constructed and governed.

As I have noted, Foucault analyzed the historical deployment of sexuality as knowledge of and power exercised over bodies and the populations to which they belonged. The hysterical woman at once personifying sexual agitation and insatiability in its anatomical lack and the need for completion through penetration by a man; the child's sexual actuality and its simultaneous latency that needed protection from distortion; the principle of an irresistible and irreducible urge that needed to be checked, by means of the "reality principle" of the couple; the sexual instinct's teleological meaning as perverted through an individual's historical adherence or biological inadequacy—the historical continuity of these four is brought to light through our various contemporaneous politics of sexuality. All of which, further, delineate the logic of compulsory heterosexuality: sexuality as the coupling of an ontological lack of genital dimorphism and complementarity with reproductive latency as its epistemological touchstone.

To be sure, within compulsory heterosexuality as a technology of government whose program is constructing the self and then regulating it, people act intentionally but not subjectively. It is not that all or most men necessarily subjectively "want" to dominate women. They just do, acting within the framework of heterosexuality, whose goal, constructing and regulating the self as *heterosexual*, emerged historically. Further, compulsory heterosexuality is exercised in a normalizing-disciplinary manner: power is exercised over bodies that are at once the object (having a male or female body) as well as the instrument (having penetrative sex with one's "complement") through which power is exercised—the subjective edification or iteration of gender through sexuality. The goal or principle according to which the performances of bodies are measured—the norm—is reproductive complementarity, the uniting of biological males and females. Finally, who exercises power in compulsory heterosexuality? In a normalizing-disciplinary order we all exercise power over one another, thus enforcing conformity to the norm; however, there are structured situations that serve as a focal point for a politics of sexuality. In them, the agency of domination lies in the one who elicits and responds (through advice, prescription, etc.) to others' accounting of their sexuality and thereby serves both a hermeneutic or truth function and a therapeutic or power function. It is a "pastoral" function, exercising power through the self-examination and confession of those over whom it is exercised.[22] This function, in earlier times a religious or

22. See Michel Foucault, "On the Beginning of the Hermeneutics of the Self," ed. Mark Blasius, *Political Theory* 21(2) (May 1993).

legal one, has now been medicalized and is exercised with reference to what is normal and what is abnormal or pathological. This domination is carried out on behalf of the normal, but its agents may be familial, pedagogical, psychiatric, or occupational, for example. Domination exists in parallel with subjection, the construction of subjects with heterosexual desire and consequent obedience to one's *own* self, as mediated through one's conscience, one's psychic authenticity, or one's sexual preference (as *it* has been shaped by the agencies of domination that constitute compulsory heterosexuality).

Sexuality, as a technology through which the modern self has come to be governed involves a uniting of the biological and the historical that allows for a principle of identity and comparability, making selfhood intelligible in our society. It is a primary principle for identity in this society, but for lesbians and gay men it is *the* principle. It is on the basis of their sexuality that they are subjected to domination, and it is through their sexual identity that they make themselves intelligible to themselves and to others. The turn-of-the-nineteenth-century "third sex" conceptualization of homosexuals as an identity remained within the rubric of gender as hypostatized by compulsory heterosexuality: the masculine/male, the feminine/female, and the psychically hermaphroditic/male or female. Contemporary lesbian and gay sexuality, perhaps, needs to be conceptualized as an assertion of the self, an insurrection of sexual subjectivity, in relation to how the technology of sexuality has historically come to invoke and govern us all. It is asserted in relation to the sexual techniques (*technē*) through which we come to know ourselves, in relation to the production and functioning of knowledge about us as sexual subjects, and in relation to the sociocultural regulation of us through our sexuality. Lesbian and gay sexuality is an insurrection, not only on the part of gender, as feminism is, but on the part of subjectivity—individuality—itself, asserted with reference to sexuality as a technology through which our selves are governed. It is, as such, a politics of our*selves* calling into question the power relations constitutive of us through our sexuality.

The Lesbian and Gay Politics of Sexuality

The historical condition of possibility for lesbian and gay politics is that sexuality has become a principal source of individual identity in our society (not just gay/straight/bi, but having a sexuality, being "sexy," having sexual "desires" as the basis for self-actualization, acting out fantasies on behalf of one's sexual desires—where desire is understood to be itself constructed by the technology of sexuality—etc.). As such, sexuality depends upon institutions, knowledges, and individuals who exercise power to elicit individual identity and then regulate it in ways ranging from advice to prescription (medical, pedagogical, psychiatric). Thus, we live in a society in which everyone has a sexuality as a principle of identity. This sexuality, however, is also an ongoing creation or invention of the self through a stylization that includes procedures upon the body—actual physical erotic techniques—as well as, and by means of, a scripting of relationships with an other or others based upon gender (explicitly, or through another trope of power, but I return to this below). Gender can be as important, only more explicitly so, in lesbian and gay sexual scripting as it is in nongay sexuality, where it can be, for nonfeminists, more or less taken as a given. It is important that the gay man is choosing another man for a sexual partner, just as it is important that the lesbian is choosing another woman, and the basis of this choice goes beyond the genital anatomy of the partner. Nongay people, too, participate somewhat in this gendered "scripting" of sexual relationships. There is, for instance, the "sensitive, straight man" of men's liberation, or the strong heterosexual woman like MacKinnon who claims that "getting pleasure [out of sex] is not my particular agenda; getting equality is. If sexual pleasure is in the way, we need to think about it."[23] But, as I demonstrated in relation to the feminist response, both to the hysterization of the female body and the political socialization of the procreative couple, feminism comprehends sexual behavior through the lens of gender—sexuality becomes an instance of inequality between biological males and females (even when, as in MacKinnon's formulations, it appears to cause it). Feminism, as such, can encompass a politics of sexuality, but in its primary concern with gender inequality and how that inequality shapes sexuality, this politics is a politics of *hetero*sexuality (or at the most, of the infiltration of heterosexual gender roles into homosexual relationships). Perhaps feminism should be more modestly conceived as problem-

23. Catharine A. MacKinnon, "Does Sexuality Have a History?" in *Discourses of Sexuality: From Aristotle to AIDS*, ed. Donna C. Stanton (Ann Arbor: University of Michigan Press, 1992), 117–36, at 134.

atizing *gender* as a structure of domination and its instantiation through subjection in interpersonal relationships.

Further, unlike the perspective of MacKinnon (and many others), a "politics of lesbian and gay sexuality" has not meant—empirically, taking even explicit collective demands as a measure (see Fig. 3)—sex acts in the service of a political agenda, "politically correct sex." Even if the "political agenda" is a good one, we can remember from the feminist sex wars of the 1980s where this leads. On the one side, critics accuse sexual practitioners of having "false consciousness" because they do not embody in their actual performance, and contribute to realizing, a future ideal (e.g., "lesbian sex without roles"). On the other side, partisans assert that lesbian and gay sex is, by its nature, inherently revolutionary ("feminism is the theory; lesbianism is the practice").[24] Fortunately, the relation between sexuality and politics is more complicated than that. I do not think one can analyze *causal* relations between a particular erotic practice and social structure (say, penetration and social inequality, or S/M and interpersonal violence in soci-

---

24. I am reminded of my late friend Guy Hocquenghem's early assertion (which he later disavowed) that gay male fucking would, by deprivatizing that most private organ of all, the anus, lead to the elimination of private property and the downfall of capitalism. Dennis Altman added that this was a good reason for gay men to rape straight men. We see a similar trajectory in Richard Mohr's argument that gay male relations are inherently equality producing and that a democratic society should therefore recognize gay men collectively as a priesthood. See Guy Hocquenghem, *Homosexual Desire*, trans. Daniella Dongoor (London: Allson & Busby, 1978), chap. 4; Dennis Altman, *The Homosexualization of America, The Americanization of the Homosexual* (New York: St. Martin's Press, 1982); and Richard Mohr, *Gay Ideas: Outing and Other Controversies* (Boston: Beacon Press, 1992), 197.

ety). To be sure, neither is lesbian and gay politics only an attempt to give us a greater realm of privacy within which sexual acts would be of no concern to the state. It is not *state* power that is primarily at issue, and it is precisely in governing us through regulating our "self" and its relations with other "selves," in what seems most "private," that the power exercised through sexuality is most effective (since we do not realize that we are being governed—being subjected within normalizing-disciplinary power relations).

Two "case studies" are suggestive with respect to this relationship between lesbian and gay sexuality and politics; they are lesbian and gay sadomasochism and lesbian butch/femme relationships. First, S/M involves an acting out of power relations in fantasy (drill sergeant/recruit, master/slave, etc.). The fantasy takes the place of real-life roles; because it is imaginary, it creates a situation where the players can go farther than they could in reality by creating a context in which they can act out their desires. It is a structured consensual situation (indeed, players speak of it as an equal exchange of power—the party ceding control, the "bottom," is actively participating in the power game and establishes with the dominant partner, the "top," whatever limits are agreed upon in advance). Although it is a fantasy situation, it could *become* real: the bondage, the instruments, the physical sensations are real. Even though the power is consensual, it could *become* nonconsensual and real. It is at this threshold between reality and fantasy that participants *understand* how a power relation "works" and how one's subjective desires allow it to work or not work, and then carry this *understanding* over into the rest of their lives. Further, such relations are reciprocal: the aim of the top (far from cruelty) is to give pleasure and set goals for the bottom; the bottom's pleasure is (apart from the physical one), like the athlete's, pushing beyond previous limits and therefore giving pleasure to the top. Michael Bronski has suggested that one of the reasons S/M became popular with gay men is that gay liberation gave them power over their own lives; given this experience for the first time, they needed a structure to understand and to learn how to use it.[25] Lesbians and gay men want to understand the heterosexist-given power relations they are enmeshed in through subjection, and they want to learn how to perceive the difference between subjection and agency by experimenting with consciously commanding and obeying, with reciprocity between top and bottom, and with the reversibility of roles. A self-described "S/M dyke of color" (and *bottom*), Tina Portillo, states that "S/M is a gift that has allowed me to deal with a lot of my hurt and pain of the past, accompanied by guilt and pain that *was not mine*. . . . I don't let anyone get away with abusing me any more. S/M has provided me with the ultimate assertiveness training. . . . I have gotten better at who I can and cannot trust, so I make saner choices in all my relationships."[26] This does not suggest that, as sympathetic

25. Michael Bronski, "A Dream Is a Wish Your Heart Makes: Notes on the Materialization of Sexual Fantasy," in *Leatherfolk: Radical Sex, People, Politics, and Practice*, ed. Mark Thompson (Boston: Alyson, 1991), 56–64. The principal lesbian-feminist anthology is playfully titled *Coming to Power*, ed. Samois (Boston: Alyson, 1987).

26. Tina Portillo, "I Get Real: Celebrating My Sadomasochistic Soul," in Thompson, *Leatherfolk*, 49–55, at 53, 55 (emphasis in original).

psychotherapists like Robert Stoller have argued,[27] such erotic practices are morally benign merely because they are *therapeutic*—because they help people overcome past psychological trauma, let them act out aggression without disruptive social consequences ("real" violence), and therefore allow them to adjust to society as it is. I suggest, one step further, that such erotic practices are a "school" for *agency*. While undertaken "in private," they can have significant political implications: through them, we learn about how we can be subjected within power relationships; at the same time, we learn how we are agents who can submit to power or, refusing, change power relationships.

The second "case study," butch/femme, has historically been persecuted by feminism as the "dupe of heterosexuality," a persecution rationalized on behalf of feminism's "androgynous imperative." Yet even if people may be "inherently androgynous" and have a "bisexual potential," the world as it is consists in institutionalized gender inequality and heterosexuality as the privileged sexual orientation, which butch/femme takes at face value. The gender-rejecting butch is rewarded for her courage by the admiration of the femme. Indeed, it is often the femme who takes care of a butch who has been battered by the world's abuse of her "gender dysfunction." This taking care occurs through a sexuality that, because the femme has created it herself to give pleasure to another woman

27. Robert Stoller, *Pain and Passion: A Psychoanalyst Explores the World of S & M* (New York: Plenum, 1991). My hypothesis needs testing with ethnographic work, of which Stoller's is a beginning; see also the primarily heterosexual ethnography by Gloria G. Brame et al., *Different Loving* (New York: Villard Books, 1993).

rather than to satisfy the demands of a man, is truly *her* creation. Further, it is her own *self-creation* through her femme sexuality. This reciprocity has been emblematized by Joan Nestle in the single word "butch-femme."[28] Like S/M, butch/femme is the creation of agency through a power game. The refusal of gender by the butch establishes agency that was preempted by gender; the femme is an active player in getting the butch to desire her and then to take control over her erotically—and this "active passivity" is ongoing.

To be sure, what I have attempted is to analyze what happens in two different kinds of same-sex relationships. I am not saying that they are paradigmatic of gay male or lesbian relationships and that somehow lesbian and gay liberation will occur if all lesbians and gay men approximate them. My point is that power relations inhere in all erotic relations because it is power, through the sexual norms and knowledges by means of which we are constituted as sexual subjects, that has inscribed the body with what is "sexy," what is "pain," and what is "pleasure"—indeed, what counts as sexual and what its use might be in living one's life. It is just that, historically, this inscription on the body has functioned to create and perpetuate gender inequality and to found heterosexuality as normal and homosexuality (and anything that is not penetrative) as in need of normalization. These two "case studies" show how, within lesbian and gay sexuality, people come to understand these power relations and

28. Joan Nestle, ed., *The Persistent Desire: A Femme-Butch Reader* (Boston: Alyson, 1992), 267.

create themselves as agents who, as such, resist how gender inequality and heterosexuality are constituted in the normalizing-disciplinary practices of everyday life—how power operates, as Foucault phrased it, on the "capillary" level.

But we have to go further. Three hypotheses are examined in the following chapters concerning the relationship between sexuality—understood here as an ethics, the creation of oneself within one's erotic relationships with others—and politics. This relationship is explored, par excellence, by lesbians and gay men because lesbian and gay sexuality is the constitution of agency within and by means of sexuality. (Understand "sexuality," again as a historically inherited technology—including knowledges, norms, and procedures like therapy or education—through which the modern self is constructed and governed.)

This lesbian and gay praxis, or politics of sexuality, involves, first, the relation of self to self in the uses one makes of one's own body. What sexuality consists in has been constructed historically as a "penetrative ethos": reproductive complementarily in a gender-stratified society is metaphorized as active versus passive, positing a congruence between one's erotic role and the power exercised through one's social role. Therefore, in this sexual ethos, what one does with one's body reveals the truth about oneself. As I have begun to demonstrate, lesbian and gay sexuality is characterized by erotic reciprocity. But, even more, it involves an ethic in which the active partner is only competent to the extent that she or he gives pleasure and in which being the passive "receiver" of pleasure is an active position, producing the possibility of giving pleasure at all and maintaining the continuity of the relationship. There may be a top and a bottom, but "who" is "what" is ambiguous and reversible in terms of power. It is not only that people may switch roles—in many cases, they are not even role-"playing" (they may understand their position as a psychic "identity"). Rather, to the extent that people invent an erotic power game, it is understood as an invention, and neither position is reinforced by social power relations as it is in heterosexuality. A further discontinuity lies explicitly within the logic of the technology of sexuality: sexuality consists in relations of *affinity* rather than biological *kinship*, and therefore involves procedures upon bodies to produce pleasure. Bodies and pleasures come first; penetration and even reproduction may then be reinscribed as a sexual-erotic technique, rather than as a cause or reason for sexuality. In an important way, lesbians, gay men, and "queers" problematize the "sex" in sexuality as derived from any natural or essential point, "truth" (genitality, sexual-dimorphic lack), upon which to ground people's relations with each other; instead of what sexual "truth" could necessitate, erotic affinities are chosen and reflect the "becoming" character of subjectivity, or agency. (It may be that a penetrative ethos of the sexed body is a result of a masculinist sexual ethics—historically written by men about men; in any case, our contemporary sexual ethics as practiced and recorded by lesbians and gay men is bound to be different.)

My second hypothesis concerns the relationship between sexuality, the self, and the other. The knowledges about sexuality posit it as an irreducible and irresistible force that, if unchecked, is dangerous to others and to oneself through dissipation. Sexuality's proximity with biological risks of disease and its imbrication with the cycle of life and death, on one hand, combine with the historical imperative of biopower, on the other hand, to make the individual body socially useful and its relations with others productive (or at least not a risk to society), so that social life appears *saturated* with sexuality that needs to be regulated. (It is precisely the fear of this sexual saturation of everyday life that has served as one of the central homophobic arguments against allowing gays and lesbians to serve openly in the U.S. military.) Lesbian and gay sexual ethics term for term transforms what "sexuality" is in a relationship between a "self" and an "other." Beyond the obvious invention of safe sex in the context of the AIDS epidemic, lesbian and gay sexuality, as I point out, demonstrates how erotic desire is produced in the context of interpersonal power relations that are then "worked through," reciprocally, to create agency. Negotiating erotic activities, the ongoing consent and the establishment of limits by the participants, and the lesbian and gay community's debate, valorization, and publication of such sexual responsibility (e.g., recent debates on gay men's "relapse" into unsafe sex, and the leather community's motto "safe, sane, and consensual") puts the lie to the image of one's loss of control within the sexual saturation of everyday life. (This loss of self-control and consequent loss of gender identity, I would conjecture, is central to "homosexual panic" among non-gays.) Indeed, the lesbian and gay community's embrace of sexuality as a *social* pleasure both makes sexuality less threatening and, through broadening the horizons of human relationships, lets individuals truly become individual—with important political consequences.

Finally, the technology of sexuality would have us come to know the truth about ourselves through our sexuality. I am concerned here with the idea—inherited from the Christian imperative to decipher all of our thoughts and confess them to authorities so that the Devil can be expunged from them—that each and every thought of ours probably has sexuality lurking within it (e.g., the "Freudian slip"). As distinct from the Christian confession, we rely upon a medical and therapeutic establishment in order to find out who we are (especially whether we are homo- or heterosexual) so that we can have, following Dr. Ruth, great sex, and feel, following the Aretha Franklin song, "like a natural woman" (or a natural man). Lesbians and gay men have, for historico-political reasons, distrusted this sexual establishment and the political economy of truth about sexuality. Instead, they have sought the truth about "our sexuality/ourselves" (to borrow from the Boston Women's Health Collective's self-help guide, *Our Bodies, Ourselves*) from each other, in ways ranging from the folk wisdom passed down through the gay or dyke bar, to lesbian, gay, and queer studies, to New York City's Children of the Rainbow Curriculum (teaching about the existence of lesbians and gay men). What is important about this knowledge is that lesbians and gays make *themselves* an object for knowledge, rather than, as was historically the case for sexuality (and for all forms of imperialism), allowing *others* to make them objects for knowledge and then buying into that interpretation. But there is more. My third hypothesis, then, is that sexuality, for lesbians and gay men, is not a realm for "truth" or scientific knowledge about the self and its desires. Rather, lesbian and gay sexuality is conducted under the sign of *art*; like the drag queen, individuals stylize their own existence by uniting the *biological* (anatomical and bodily modification, musculature, physiological function, sensation, surgical transsexualism) with the *historical* (the gym body, the pierced body, the tattooed body, "playing" with gender, costume and dress, role-playing/power games as erotic stimulant, etc.). Sexuality becomes a stylization of the self in order to have relations with others through giving each other bodily pleasure. And it is by this disconnection with sexual science and its production of a discourse of truth about sexual practices that lesbian and gay subjection through the technology of sexuality is, if not elided, reversed. Lesbian and gay sexuality involves creating ethical agency *through*, rather than remaining a reflex *of*, the organization of power by the normalizing-disciplinary practices of sexuality. And this agency is in an aesthetic or *queer* mode rather than in one relying upon a universal truth about human nature and the necessary relations among human bodies.

Thus, this praxis—in the relation of self to self in the sexual uses of the body; in the relation between sexuality, the self, and others; and in the relation between sexuality, the self, and truth—allows for the creation of agency through sexuality, that then allows for the creation of historical agency in lesbian and gay politics. As such, this sexual praxis or *erotics* is paradigmatic of the politics of sexuality in our time.

Chapter 3

Sexuality, Subjectivity, and Political Identity

Your body is a battleground

from a poster designed by Barbara Kruger publicizing the national march on Washington, D.C., for reproductive freedom, April 9, 1989

Sexual relationships are contiguous with and part of other relationships—those of the writer to pen and paper, of the body-builder to weights. . . . The bedroom is no more the privileged site of sexuality than any other space; sexuality and desire are part of the intensity and passion of life itself.

Elizabeth Grosz, *Refiguring Lesbian Desire*

Sexuality, as it has emerged historically, is a technology we use for having relationships with one another. Through this technology, individuals are constructed as subjects "with a sexuality" and are then regulated by norms of "compulsory heterosexuality" that are justified by a reflection upon the nature of the human individual and sociality. Lesbians and gays call into question, transform, and further elaborate this technology of government by problematizing sexual subjectivity in the creation of lesbian and gay identity and a social movement based upon it; by problematizing how compulsory heterosexuality is enforced through norms, laws, and social institutions in asserting a relational right; and by problematizing as *political* that is, as a qualifying rationale for the exercise of power, the social ontology and epistemology of compulsory heterosexuality.

Chapters 3, 4, and 5 examine these three aspects or moments of lesbian and gay politics. In this chapter, thus, I analyze how "lesbian" and "gay" have come into existence historically as categories of political subjectivity. I address the historical conditions of possibility for the emergence of "lesbian" and "gay" persons; how, through their sexual experience, lesbians and gays constitute themselves *as* persons; and what the political significance of this "coming out" as lesbian or gay is.

A Genealogy of Gay and Lesbian Identity

Recall that sexuality has been historically constituted as a technology of government, government through sexuality, in four areas of governmental concern: the female body because of its significance for woman's social role and the future of the species; the sexual conduct of children because of their status of possessing, *in potentia*, socially significant sexuality; the couple, to which was attributed both health and procreative responsibilities; and, finally, sexual behaviors or pleasures that were considered a perverse or anomalous expression of the sexual instinct and in need of correction ("the homosexual" came to personify a whole cluster of these, including sodomy, inversion, pederasty, and "psychic hermaphroditism"). While there has been homoerotic behavior of individuals throughout history and in most cultures, as well as people who have self-identified on the basis of primary or exclusive homosexuality it was not until the middle of the nineteenth century that physicians and psychiatrists conceptualized a homosexual type of person (one whose sexual instinct was perverted into same-sex object choice) and, through the use of urban police surveillance records (among other statistical measures), conceptualized homosexual person*s* that could comprise a population of homosexuals targeted for regulation by the state. Thus, it is in the context of this primarily administrative and therapeutic concern that we must view the creation of a distinctive homosexual or contemporary "lesbian" and "gay" identity. To be sure, while there is debate among historians as to when a distinctive and self-conscious male homoerotic way of life emerged, what is not disputed is that the invention of the term "homosexual" was preceded by, and was an attempt to label scientifically and hence govern, individuals who participated in a distinctive urban way of life.[1] There was, therefore, a bio-

1. See John Boswell, *Christianity, Social Tolerance, and Homosexuality: Gay People in Western Europe from the Beginning of the Christian Era to the Fourteenth Century* (Chicago: University of Chicago Press, 1980), chap. 1, for a historical overview of gay self-consciousness in the West. This section of my book is meant to briefly historically contextualize the development of lesbian and gay ethics. For a detailed documentary genealogy, see Mark Blasius and Shane Phelan, *We Are Everywhere: A Historical Sourcebook in Gay and Lesbian Politics* (New

political construction of a population of homosexuals at the same time and by means of the diagnosis of homosexuality as a perversion of the sexual instinct that was treatable, anatomo-politically, on an individual basis. This construction of modern homosexuality "made possible a 'reverse' discourse: homosexuality began to speak on its own behalf, to demand that its legitimacy or 'naturality' be acknowledged, often in the same vocabulary, using the same categories by which it was radically disqualified."[2] Contemporary lesbian and gay identity is heir to this reverse or counterdiscourse because, as an urban gay subculture developed and became targeted for regulation by the state through medicine, psychiatry, and the judicial and educational systems, the reverse discourse by homosexuals themselves initially resisted from within the categories and institutions through which power was exercised. For example, Kertbeny invented the term "homosexual" specifically to argue that homosexuality was a medical condition and therefore

---

York: Routledge, 1995). For the development of lesbian and gay group consciousness, and the emergence of homosexuality as a sociomedical "problem," see Martin Bauml Duberman, Martha Vicinus, and George Chauncey, Jr., eds., *Hidden from History: Reclaiming the Gay and Lesbian Past* (New York: NAL Books, 1989); and Barry D. Adam, *The Rise of a Gay and Lesbian Movement* (Boston: Twayne, 1987), 15. For a history of female romantic friendships, see Lillian Faderman, *Surpassing the Love of Men* (New York: William Morrow, 1981). For historical studies of this emergent way of life, see Alan Bray, *Homosexuality in Renaissance England* (London: Gay Men's Press, 1982); Guido Ruggiero, *The Boundaries of Eros: Sex Crime and Sexuality in Renaissance Venice* (New York: Oxford University Press, 1985), chap. 6; and Randolph Trumbach, "Gender and the Homosexual Role in Modern Western Culture: The 18th and 19th Centuries Compared," in *Homosexuality, Which Homosexuality?* by D. Altman et al. (London: GMP Publishers, 1989).

2. Michel Foucault, *The History of Sexuality*, vol. 1, *An Introduction*, trans. Robert Hurley (New York: Pantheon Books, 1978), 101.

should not be subject to criminalization as sodomy, an act believed contrary to Scripture. The nineteenth- and early twentieth-century German gay sex researcher Magnus Hirschfeld argued for tolerance based upon his belief in the innate character of homosexuality; his perspective foreshadowed those of today's sociobiologists. Contemporary gay and lesbian thinkers sometimes use the language of liberalism to argue that, while the majority may be offended by homosexuality, homosexuals should be treated like any other minority, without discrimination or violence, so long as the offensive erotic *behavior* is kept "private." However, in spite of its historical construction as a reverse or counterdiscourse, the early homosexual (later, after the 1969 New York City Stonewall Riots, "gay") discourse was a manifestation of a new way of life, pathologized and thereby targeted for state regulation. Although the way of life preceded its conceptualization as engaged in by "homosexuals," pathologization resulted in a political movement that ultimately further elaborated the nascent urban subculture.[3]

The urban gay way of life emerged primarily as a male phenomenon until the twentieth century. There is, thus, an important difference in the historical development of lesbian and gay male identity. Except for the few women who passed as men—even marrying other women—to avail themselves of the economic

3. I am not arguing that there were no self-identified homosexual persons prior to the nineteenth century, before which everybody was polymorphously perverse. I am, rather, analyzing the development of a gay movement and a gay politics that is made historically possible through the way power has come to be exercised in the modern age—as biopower.

opportunities open to men, most women could not enter the wage-labor market throughout the nineteenth century. Instead, they were relegated to the domestic sphere, economically dependent on men. It was only toward the end of the century that women, entering into wage labor, were able to release themselves from the heterosexual kinship system and make exclusive homosexuality possible, pointing toward different domestic relationships and social networks. This resulted, during the twentieth century, in an emerging lesbian world, existing, for example, "among female faculty of women's colleges, among single working women and prostitutes of boardinghouse districts in large cities, among entertainers in Harlem, and along the fringes of bohemian communities in places such as New York City's Greenwich Village" as the historian John D'Emilio has traced its emergence. To be sure, "romantic friendships" among women existed during the nineteenth century in Europe and the United States. But, as Lillian Faderman has shown, these relationships tended to take place within the existing kinship system (in part because sexuality for women was only conceived functionally, for procreation or to please one's husband) and therefore were not realized as an alternative to it that could provide the basis for a distinctive social identity.[4] (A parallel to this was male homoeroticism, documented since the sixteenth century within households between master and servant, although *it* was overtly genital and thus

4. John D'Emilio, "The Making and Unmaking of Minorities," in *Making Trouble: Essays on Gay History, Politics, and the University* (New York: Routledge, 1992), 184; Faderman, *Surpassing the Love of Men.*

persecuted as sodomy.)[5] It appears that when, because of the possibility of financial independence in wage labor, romantic friendship began to elide male control based upon marriage and heterosexuality, it became a pathologized identity—lesbianism and tribadism, for example.

The evolution of lesbian and gay identity depended upon a number of common factors, even though the specific historical development was somewhat different for lesbians and gay men. First, it was necessary for homoerotic relationships to be able to take place outside the structure of heterosexual kinship. This meant that social networks based on homoerotic interest could develop independently of other existing relationships, that exclusive homosexuality could become possible, and that homoerotic bonding could make up an "endogamous" social formation with collective self-awareness (including styles of dress, argot, social spaces for meeting others, social networks, and, later, cultural and political organizations) such that it could be transmitted across time.[6] This constituted the gay male subculture in existence from the sixteenth to the twentieth centuries and the lesbian subculture from the late nineteenth to the twentieth. Increasing political repression in the twentieth century, justified by medical expertise and using legal techniques of enforcement (statutes prohibiting sodomy, public lewdness, and sexual solicitation, absence of civil-rights protection against social discrimi-

5. See Bray, *Homosexuality in Renaissance England*; and Ruggiero, *The Boundaries of Eros*.

6. Barry Adam, "Structural Foundations of the Gay World," *Comparative Studies in Society and History* 27(4) (1985): 658.

nation), resulted in the formation of a political movement. From World War II until the Stonewall Riots of 1969, when this repression was greatest, lesbians and gay men worked together in the same or allied organizations. Even though the term "gay" was adopted in the early 1970s as a self-chosen political label (it meant the opposite of the pathological label and could include women and men—as "queer" is meant to do today, while co-opting a stereotype), the emergence of lesbian feminism at roughly the same moment made tenuous a nascent collective identity derived from repression of homosexuality alone. The idea of the lesbian continuum, "a range—through each woman's life and throughout history—of woman identified experience; not simply the fact that a woman has or had or consciously desired genital sexual experience with another woman," an influential formulation of this political ideology, tended to link female homosexuals with the plight of all women more than with the plight of male homosexuals.[7] Are lesbians' concerns closer to the concerns of all women than to those of gay men? Should lesbians be conceived of as the vanguard of women's liberation and therefore, when separatist, a female priesthood akin to Richard Mohr's vision for gay men in relation to democratic culture? Will nonlesbian feminists trade off lesbian concerns for respectability and acceptance by the political main-

---

7. The "lesbian continuum" is from Adrienne Rich, "Compulsory Heterosexuality and Lesbian Existence," in *Powers of Desire: The Politics of Sexuality*, ed. Ann Snitow, Christine Stansell, and Sharon Thompson (New York: Monthly Review Press, 1983), 192. For a discussion of the tensions between lesbianism and feminism, see Shane Phelan, *Identity Politics: Lesbian Feminism and the Limits of Community* (Philadelphia: Temple University Press, 1989).

stream? These are principal tensions of lesbian and gay identity today in ideology and political strategy, as well as within the lived experience of lesbians and gay men in their relations with each other. While we cannot resolve the tension through writing about it, it has become clear that a collaborative movement has only been possible to the extent that the movement slogan "you cannot fight heterosexism without fighting sexism at the same time" is operationalized. To the extent that it is, it creates the possibility for *social* relations of equality—not necessarily intimate friendships—between lesbians and gay men within what has come to be called the lesbian and gay commmunity. (The question of whether such a community exists is addressed in Chapter 5.)

Further, the demonstrable successes in legislation and judicial cases, at least in the United States, have come about through a collaboration between lesbians and gay men in the major organizations that comprise the institutional component of the social movement. In New York City's Manhattan alone, the Lesbian and Gay Community Services Center provides office space for lesbian and gay organizations and meeting space for ninety-eight different groups that hold events every month (this is not to mention providing space for organizations that do not meet so regularly). There are also a number of lesbian and gay political organizations and AIDS-service programs that occupy all or the greater part of several Manhattan office buildings. In addition, the Hetrick-Martin Institute for the Protection of Lesbian and Gay Youth offers social services for young people and operates, in conjunction with the New York City Board of Education, a lesbian and gay high school, the Harvey Milk School. Also, the City University of New York has created a lesbian and gay studies center that offers colloquia and public symposia, and research fellowships; Columbia University followed with a seminar series; and the Lesbian Herstory Archives and the Gay History Archives are repositories for documentation of the modern lesbian and gay movement. There are, as well, art galleries, a repertory theater company, radio programs, two television networks and numerous cable-television programs serving New York City's gays and lesbians.

To be sure, there is a great degree of separatism within what I am calling the lesbian and gay movement, both institutionally and interpersonally. However, for the purpose of a political theory of sexuality, I am conceptualizing the way in which institutional change has been brought about through the collaboration of lesbians and gay men on the basis of how they have been commonly oppressed, their homosexuality. For whatever else might mobilize them politically as individuals and as members of same-sex groups—rape, gender stereotypes, abortion rights, racial or cultural discrimination—it is their sexual subjection that has incited the historical creation of the political identities of lesbian or gay and the movement that gives these identities historical agency.

Erotics: From Subjection to Agency

Lesbian and gay sexuality involves the creation of agency within and through erotic practices. This means both a desubjectification of homophobia within individuals and a positive creation of selfhood. To the extent that these also take a *public* form in what is called "coming out" (where "public" is understood both as being socially visible as gay or lesbian and as introducing a change in the public power that constitutes heterosexist domination), compulsory heterosexuality is displaced. I call this creation of agency through sexuality *erotics.* In the next section, I analyze its possible consequence in the creation of political subjectivity through coming out. Here I discuss how lesbians and gay men work through their subjection in the four moments of ethical self-constitution through erotics.

First, the part of oneself that one is concerned about, that one is working on, is one's sexuality, understood as one's erotic choices (that would include object choice, what counts as erotic pleasure, what motivates one—feelings, desires, what one thinks is "sexy," etc.). To be sure, lesbians and gays are not the only people who comprehend themselves ethically through their sexuality. In the history of sexual practices, the Greeks' ethical substance was the *aphrodisia* and the Christians' was the *flesh.* Also historically, it is within the context of contemporary heterosexist domination and homophobic subjection that lesbians and gays have had to pay most attention, ethically, to their sexuality; hence, erotics "orients" their lives. Thus, lesbians and gays have to first figure out that they are such and then de-link their sexual choices from what has been given to them culturally (reproductive genital heterosexuality and gender complementarity) in order to create a new ethical substance, what "works" for them, their lesbian or gay sexuality.

Why, second, do we care about our sexuality? We

are invoked by procedures of subjection through which the human subject is constructed and then managed, to recognize our sexuality as, say, homo, hetero, or bi. To the extent we discover it is possible to be "gay" or "lesbian" (as distinct from being an isolated, sinful, or diseased "homosexual"), those in the lesbian and gay community serve as a source of sexual information, as well as provide criteria for recognizing and working on that aspect of ourselves that is our sexuality. The community serves, for example, by providing critiques of heterosexism and homophobia on the part of one's peers through written and orally transmitted forms of knowledge—philosophical, fictional, scientific, autobiographical and biographical—derived from lesbian and gay life, and by being constituted through social networks and formal institutions (publishing and media, community centers, lesbian/gay studies, recreational, and commercial facilities) that enable us to work on our sexuality and invent ourselves. Equally valuable (and in the case of gay men perhaps, more important than, say, "think pieces" in gay and lesbian magazines and gay and lesbian literature generally) is *erotica* (a better term than pornography, in a gay and lesbian context, since here the fantasy images do not foster the inequality of women with men). Erotica is indispensable to recognizing one's sexual feelings, learning that there are others who share them, and experimenting with and testing one's own physical and psychic limits. According to the lesbian feminist Pat Califia, the value of erotica is that it offers what lesbians—and all women—need to constitute their own freedom: "a vision of that woman of the future, including her ideas about what 'sexy' means and looks like, and what 'pleasure' is, and what it's worth."[8] Further, its role and value in the socialization of often isolated gay youth cannot be underestimated in the formation of a subculture and consequent political movement.

Third, how do we use our sexuality in living our lives? This aspect of self-constitution involves how we use sexuality in creating our selves through specific erotic practices and through the kinds of relationships we form based upon our sexuality (e.g., a lesbian's circle of intimates and their intimates, gay male fuckbuddies, former lovers, AIDS carepartners), as well as how we use such relationships to again further elaborate our sexuality (e.g., how lesbian and gay couples integrate sexual freedom into their relationships). In an argument parallel to this one, Sarah Lucia Hoagland distinguishes between patriarchal "sex" and a lesbian "erotic" and "desire" that gets fragmented and needs mending. This can be achieved by infusing lesbian desire into one's everyday social life; demystifying the erotic, seeing it not as a loss of control but as a source of connection with others; "overlap[ping] the concepts of 'friend' and 'lover' "; and recognizing the connection between humor and the erotic (what I would call sexual playfulness).[9] Further, the narrow meaning of coming out also lies here—self-disclosure is a specific,

8. Pat Califia, *Macho Sluts* (Boston: Alyson, 1988), 14. Furthermore, the narrative content of lesbian and gay erotica involves the eroticization of everyday life, as well as the ironic use of gender roles, both of which are indispensable to ethical self-formation. See also the analyses of gay male erotica in biweekly columns by Mingus [Michael Denneny] in the *New York Native* during 1986 and 1987, especially "Through the Looking Glass" (July 7–13, 1986).

9. Sarah Lucia Hoagland, *Lesbian Ethics: Toward New Value* (Palo Alto, Calif.: Institute for Lesbian Studies, 1988), 164–77.

socially visible practice with regard to one's self-creation through sexuality. However, lesbian and gay erotics involves relational techniques that have a certain specificity. This is so by virtue of the situation of lesbians and gays within sexuality as a technology of government as it has come to be historically constituted as compulsory heterosexuality.

■ Erotics is "public" in the sense that it occurs in places of sociality, so that any distinction between sexuality and sociality is made relative. Sexual relations can be immediately translated into social relations, and social relations can be understood as always potentially sexual relations. The existence of sexual/social institutions (lesbian and gay sex clubs, women's music festivals, bathhouses, gyms and athletic events, gay or lesbian resorts, etc.) makes sexual relations both regulated and open. Rather than being a parenthesis within one's life, one's "private sex life," sexuality becomes integrated into all of one's relationships. This results, not in "promiscuity," but in the integration of sexuality and friendship (taking it away from the exclusive province of either the one-night stand or the monogamous couple) and in the integration of sexual health into communal life (a reality that saved gay men's lives from the outset of the AIDS epidemic).[10] Thus, rather than as a prelude to marriage

10. The lesbian and gay community, as I discuss in Chapter 5, allows for the development of a sexual ethics where "regulation" is at once interpersonal and communal (but not necessarily legal), allowing for a constant reflection upon one's relation to oneself. Examples of such "regulation" include debates about sexuality in lesbian and gay media; publication of safe-sex guidelines; distribution of condoms, dental dams, and lube; the employment of "lifeguards" in sexual institutions; friendship networks as "safety nets" for potential or actual

or coupling, lesbians and gay men use their sexuality throughout the course of life to create diverse relationships and to integrate sexual freedom within relationships as a source of revitalization, innovation, and self-invention. As such, lesbian and gay sexuality can be a celebration of eros pure and simple, regardless of whether there is "love," and therefore need not trespass on the trust and fidelity of any specific kind of relationship.

- Role-playing—whether drag and gender play involving hyperbole, transgression, and the like, or the roles of butch/femme, top/bottom, S/M, and so on—is complementary. But because the roles are *chosen* by the players (and are therefore reversible—can be un-chosen) and are not frozen either through institutions or through a psychic "lack," they relativize power relations that inhere in social relations—especially gender, but also those of race or ethnicity, age, and class. Such relativization of racial power can be observed in the erotic drawings of Tom of Finland, for example; in the case of class, in butch/femme and S/M relationships; and, in the case of age, in intergenerational (not pedophilic) relationships, where the age differential can fuel an erotic reversal of the actual social power roles. The work of the psychiatrist Robert Stoller on "perversion as subversion" is suggestive for

---

partnering; and venues where the relationship between one's sexuality and the rest of one's life is specifically addressed and integrated, such as workshops, religious institutions, and professional and special-interest organizations. (The best definition of promiscuity I have heard is the one current in Gay Men's Health Crisis safer-sex workshops: "promiscuous is anyone who has more sex than I do.")

analysis of the creation of agency through erotic role-playing and erotics generally.[11]

- The use of sexuality for purposes other than reproduction, and not necessarily with a genital-centric focus—that is, using every part of the body as a sexual instrument in order to achieve the greatest intensification of pleasure possible, alone or with partners, and for the partners to give pleasure *reciprocally*—results in a sexual ethic of integrating the pleasure of the other into one's own pleasure: "I get off getting you off."

Lesbian and gay erotic techniques thus relativize sexuality and elide compulsory heterosexuality in three ways. First, there is a relativization of social and sexual relations, of who can have sex with whom, when, and where. Erotics de-links sexuality from "true love" and the monogamously idealized couple while it integrates it within the fabric of social life: sexuality becomes a *social* pleasure (like potluck dinners and participation in amateur sports). Second, there is a relativization of social power relations

---

11. For exemplary analyses of and materials about these erotic phenomena, see the interviews on racial images in the documentary videos of Tom of Finland, *Daddy and the Muscle Academy* (1992) and *Boots, Biceps, and Bulges: The Life and Works of Tom of Finland* (1988). See also *The Persistent Desire: A Butch-Femme Reader*, ed. Joan Nestle (Boston: Alyson, 1992); Madeline Davis and Elizabeth Kennedy, *Boots of Leather, Slippers of Gold* (New York: Routledge, 1993); *Coming to Power*, ed. Samois (Boston: Alyson, 1987); *Leather Folk*, ed. Mark Thompson (Boston: Alyson, 1991); Brian Pronger, *The Arena of Masculinity: Sports, Homosexuality, and the Meaning of Sex* (New York: St. Martin's Press, 1990); and Susie Bright, *Susie Sexpert's Lesbian Sex World* (Pittsburgh: Cleis Press, 1990). Robert Stoller's hypothesis, tested against case studies of intrapsychic S/M experience, can be applied to accounts of lesbian and gay erotic relationships; Robert Stoller, *Pain and Pleasure: A Psychoanalyst Explores the World of S & M* (New York: Plenum, 1991), 45–47.

through the choice of erotic roles and, indeed, the bracketing of one's own social identity through an erotics that can relativize actual social power relations while working through, erotically, the roles by which they operate. Finally, there is the relativization of body parts and of what counts as sexual, of what is sexually "permitted" and "forbidden," of what it is possible to do with one's sexuality.

Fourth, and last, what is the kind of being to which one aspires through one's erotics? In fashioning oneself, one aspires to become an *agent* by means of one's erotic relationships with others. Constituting oneself as subject of one's actions, constituting one's own freedom, is what ethics is; doing so with scrupulous deliberateness, an ascesis in and through the lesbian and gay community, results in an ethos of self-invention that one shares with others. (I discuss a lesbian and gay ethos in detail in Chapter 5.) This is the goal of coming out—crafting a way of life through one's homoerotics.

Erotic desire is itself inextricably enmeshed with power relations—indeed, desire is an aspect of the subject that has been constructed through a psychological and medical heterosexualization from the earliest age, as I pointed out in regard to the sexualization of childhood. Lesbian and gay desire takes this quasi-natural aspect of the subject and, through "events" of pleasure (erotic techniques, sexual "scenes"), transmutes value by means of community-based erotic culture and remaps the heterosexualized body with the goal of at once decolonizing it and using it as a touchstone for inventing and continuously reinventing the self. Even if this is conceived as an innate homosexuality eventually breaking through a culturally conditioned heterosexuality, it is a creation of the self against the void within which one finds oneself when first discovering erotic feeling for the same sex. One might say that, instead of Aretha Franklin's "You Make Me Feel Like a Natural Woman," a gay and lesbian romantic anthem would be more like the semidrag, AIDS-taken Sylvester's gay disco hit, "You Make Me Feel Mighty Real."

Silence = Death: Coming Out and the Creation of the Self

First I traced, genealogically, the historical emergence of the categories "lesbian" and "gay." These are political categories in the sense that they exist as a function of a political movement. They developed historically as a defense against and a rejection of compulsory heterosexuality—a structure of domination that enforces heterosexuality as normative—and against procedures of subjection that create homophobic subjects (even those who may engage in homoerotic relations). Then I analyzed how, through their erotics, such subjects "reverse" the procedures of homophobic subjection. This comes about through the use of the body to invent a new relation of oneself to oneself by means of networks of relationships, institutions, and types of relationships that challenge the structure of human relations that constitutes heterosexist domination. Lesbian and gay, however, in addition to being individual sexual identities are also affirmations of a way of living using the technology of sexuality while transforming it—displacing the historical residue of compulsory heterosexuality. This is accomplished through what is called "coming out," and it is the condition of possibility for political identity and historical agency as a movement.

The interaction between the use of sexuality in constituting the self and the formation of a collective identity through coming out can be comprehended, in one example, through the development of gay male sexual practices and identity, and their transformation during the AIDS epidemic. The significance of this development and transformation cannot be understated. According to Robert Padgug, a historian of the gay movement:

> Gay institutions devoted to sexual activity—bars, baths, backrooms, public spaces—were of great importance, although they hardly exhaust the content of the gay male community. The fundamental link among gay men, without which a gay male community could not have developed, was, after all, sexual. But it is important to understand that these institutions have historically represented far more than places to have sex, and have developed a greater symbolic and social significance to the gay community than have their non-gay counterparts. For decades they represented the only public spaces that could in any sense be termed homosexual and in which homosexuals could discover others like them within a homosexual world, despite frequent police raids and moral crusades. . . . [An] immense role [was] played by these spaces in that complicated double process of "coming out"—that is, entering the homosexual world as well as publicly committing oneself to one's homosexuality. . . .
>
> It is not surprising, therefore, that when gay

> people asserted themselves and their right to exist in the gay liberation of the 1960s, these sexual institutions expanded astronomically and the room for sexual experimentation and creativity also expanded as an expression of gay identity, as a protest against the suppression of homosexuality, and as a genuine attempt to fashion a new society under new conditions of freedom. The public nature of much of this sexuality became another expression of the manner in which *gay male sex was a product of a community, not merely of a group of preexisting homosexual individuals.*[12]

This passage shows also the interplay between individual and collective constitution in gay male life. Male homosexual sexual practices created a community; the existence of the community then transformed the identities of its members as gay. Those involved then reshaped their sexuality (ethical substance) through techniques (ethical practice) learned from one another in the context of *gay* community values and norms of sexual and social comportment (mode of subjection), resulting in what I discuss later as an ethos (the telos of ethical self-constitution). Further, it was in the context of the AIDS epidemic that, because of their collective identity, their institutions, and their knowledge of risk factors, gay men were again able to reshape the sexual practices that had served as the basis for forming this identity in the first instance. The epidemic did not in any way weaken their political

12. Robert Padgug, "More than the Story of a Virus: Gay History, Gay Communities, and AIDS," *Radical America* 21(2–3): 39–40 (emphasis in original).

identity; in fact, as I demonstrate in Chapter 4, it was the context within which this identity was elaborated and strengthened even more.

Similarly, lesbians understand themselves as rejecting *their* subjected identity as woman, inherited from their role in heterosexuality, for a different identity as lesbian, generated through a transvaluing of desire and lesbian erotics. Thus, in the words of Sarah Lucia Hoagland:

> [I] mean to suggest that we move among each other as "lesbians," not as "women." . . . Once it was enough to just come out as a lesbian. Now we know better. We understand that being lesbian at most creates the possibility of a certain kind of female agency.

She asks

> whether sex is a purely biological phenomenon like eating and drinking and sleeping, or whether it is something whose meaning emerges through an institutional context, as is the case with breakfasting, dining, or going to potluck dinners.
>
> Thus, understanding sexuality is not just understanding a "drive" but understanding the context, indeed the institutions, which gives our urges and responses depth of meaning.

> Our desire in a certain sense is a microcosm of the macrocosm of our oppression: it has been erased and/or used against us to such an extent that we turn against ourselves and suppress it; and yet when we do manage to overcome what's been done with our lesbian desire and explore it in joy and discovery, it comes out all prepro-

> grammed by the patriarchal institution of sexuality and still erasing, fragmenting, destroying.
>
> When each of us came out, we invoked lesbian desire and we turned our attention to lesbian existence. It was a choice, a judgment. . . . Our lesbian energy emerges from an integration of our selves and our interactions with each other. And that integration involves both judgment of context and interaction with subjects. As such, that choice is political.[13]

Coming out refers, then, to an ontological recognition of the self by the self. It involves a re-cognition of one's sexuality (whether subjectively understood as a Freudian bisexual potential, an innate homoeroticism, or an existential choice or imperative) and—starting from this recognition—working on one's sexuality so that the self appears and becomes. Coming out is also *the* fundamental political act. It involves rejecting one's own subjection (being "in the closet," "passing," treating others homophobically, etc.) that is the product of historical processes of domination by heterosexism. It further involves, through recognition of and by other lesbian and gay people, cognizing or thinking over and thinking differently of oneself and one's relations with others—creating oneself under what thereby become *different* historical conditions.

The politicalness and creation of personal and then historical agency that coming out is lies in its transformation of what one writer, refashioning a concept from Vaclav Havel, terms the "heterosexual panorama." The institutional organization of heterosexu-

13. Hoagland, *Lesbian Ethics*, 9, 166, 175–76, 177.

ality and the creation of subjects who serve that organization result in, if not a seamless web, at least the expectation of heterosexuality and the invisibility of homosexuality. As people are controlled in former totalitarian societies through "a system of appearances exhibiting and reinforcing certain values endorsed by the regime," so the heterosexual panorama is "the backdrop of daily life in which everyone is assumed to be hetero [and] gays are allowed to exist only by blending into the background." Analogous to Havel's post-totalitarian system, there

> is the heterosexual panorama exhibiting the officially endorsed sexual values, the opposition between these and the authentic selves of those living under the system, the false identity that people are obliged to maintain, the act of rebellion—the assertion of one's authentic self in the face of the system—and the punishments for breaking the rules of the game and claiming one's true identity and dignity.[14]

Institutionally, homosexuality is erased from or distorted within educational curricula and the mass media, denied status in or as family, identified with gender dysfunction, and "tolerated" (if at all) as second-class humanity—all of which is legitimized either by legal prohibition or lack of protection, as well as by religious and moral exhortation.

In a complementary way, all of this encourages individuals, by tacit but firm forms of rewards and punishments, not to "break ranks," to go along participat-

14. Jerry McCarthy, "The Closet and the Politics of Outing," paper supplied to me by Richard A. Mohr, 17.

ing in the panorama, the collective belief (or alibi) that lesbians and gays do not exist or, if they do, only do so in negative, stereotypical ways. "Coming out of the closet" is like blowing the whistle on the panorama. It is through the cumulative, strategically directed performances of coming out that the procedures of subjection disciplining the norms of heterosexuality are reversed, and the normalizing-disciplinary order—the panorama—of compulsory heterosexuality is transformed. This would include, for example, the demand to have lesbian and gay families represented in elementary school curricula, and the coming out of their children as such, the persistent coming out of adolescents, and their support by friendship networks and social service agencies in resistance to an educational, familial, and peer-based normative order that molds—subjects them—as heterosexual. As such a reversal, coming out places a (strategic and historical) limit, through the freedom that inheres in the ethical constitution of the gay or lesbian subject, on the exercise of power—government through sexuality. Coming out is, therefore, quintessentially political. One can exist "passively," say, as an ethnic minority or a woman; however, to exist as gay or lesbian one must *do* something to exist as such. And like whistle-blowing, conscientious objection, and civil disobedience, doing something, coming out, affects the normative fabric of human life as we experience it today.

One does not come out once and for all, however, and coming out is not just a disclosure of one's gay or lesbian identity to others. Rather than being an end state in which one exists as an "out" person, coming out is a process of becoming, a lifelong learning of how to become (and of inventing the meaning of being) a lesbian or a gay man in this historical moment. A lesbian and gay community can only exist to the extent that people come out into it, to the extent that they understand themselves and identify themselves to others as lesbian and gay. These acts of self-disclosure (and, as I shall point out, public self-creation) and the mutual recognition attendant upon them create a community that lies beyond both a historically prior gay or lesbian subculture and a mere "lifestyle enclave" based upon "the narcissism of similarity" in patterns of leisure and consumption.[15]

The process character of coming out can be gleaned from some of the "meanings in use" that define it: coming out to those who did not know one is gay or lesbian; coming out by holding hands with one's lover in a public place (an action that frequently elicits lesbian and gay bashing); coming out in a lesbian/gay pride march or by joining a lesbian or gay organization; coming out professionally by writing a novel with a lesbian or gay theme, through one's choice of research topics, or by teaching a lesbian-or gay-oriented lesson or course; coming out as a PWA (person living with AIDS) or as being HIV-positive, or as someone affected by AIDS and doing something about it; coming out by crossing a sexual frontier, by having a new experience of the body and what counts

15. This conception of lifestyle is that of Robert N. Bellah, et al., *Habits of the Heart: Individualism and Commitment in American Life* (Berkeley and Los Angeles: University of California Press, 1985), as cited in Stephen O. Murray, "Components of Gay Community in San Francisco," in *Gay Culture in America: Essays from the Field*, ed. Gilbert Herdt (Boston: Beacon Press, 1991), 114.

as sexual pleasure, or by a ritual that marks acceptance into, for example, the leather culture, as leather people speak of it—"a second coming out . . . rest[ing] on an experience of intense personal discovery and acceptance . . . a form of birth, a replacement of one world and a good deal of its values with those more attuned to the demands of a Gay person."[16] Obviously not all of these uses of coming out are exclusive to lesbian and gay existence—Magic Johnson "came out" as HIV-positive (as Arthur Ashe was "outed"), and there has been enough linguistic slippage that people now speak of "coming out" as incest survivors or recovering substance abusers. However, what is specific to lesbian and gay existence about coming out is that the aspect of the self that one is concerned about recognizing in oneself is one's *sexuality* as it has been addressed by mechanisms of power that create heterosexual subjects. Coming out at once reverses those mechanisms and uses them for affirmative relations with others. Gay and lesbian politics often involves the ironic cooptation of cultural symbols of power as part of a process of "empowerment"—constitution of agency within power relations in order to change those relations. "You call me queer? Yes, I am queer; I love other queers and we are building a queer nation and a queer planet." Just as the "Silence = Death" logo is an ironic co-optation of the Nazis' pink triangle and provides a reminder of it and a basis for gay and lesbian affirmation and AIDS activism (Figs. 1 and 2), the reverse discourse of coming out

16. Geoff Mains, *Urban Aboriginals: A Celebration of Leathersexuality* (San Francisco: Gay Sunshine Press, 1984), 24, 25.

is an ironic transvaluation of values that are enforced through sexuality.

Subjection within the political logic of compulsory heterosexuality involves the construction of abnormal, unnatural, unhealthy, and sinful subjects. Within this historically inherited technology of sexuality, gay and lesbian identity is a procedure for such subjects to constitute themselves as individual and social agents and, in so doing, create a political identity. As such, coming out is not, strictly speaking, freedom "from" the heterosexual panorama; rather, it is a constitution of individual and collective historical agency within this system that then transforms it. Coming out is not freedom *from* power exercised through sexuality; rather, it questions the truth claims by which compulsory heterosexuality is enabled, and transforms *how* power is exercised in this society. Put a different way, gay and lesbian *lives*—understood both as social visibility and (what I analyze in Chapter 4) as the claim of a right—challenge how cultural norms constitute heterosexist domination and how normalizing-disciplinary power is exercised through sexual subjection.

Conclusion: After Sexuality, Erotics?

Sexuality—or, better, in a lesbian or gay context, *erotics*—is the principal ethical category for lesbians and gay men. It is through their erotic relationships that subjectivity is constituted, that the lesbian or gay man constitutes her—or himself as an agent of actions in relation to an other or others. Lesbian and gay erotics

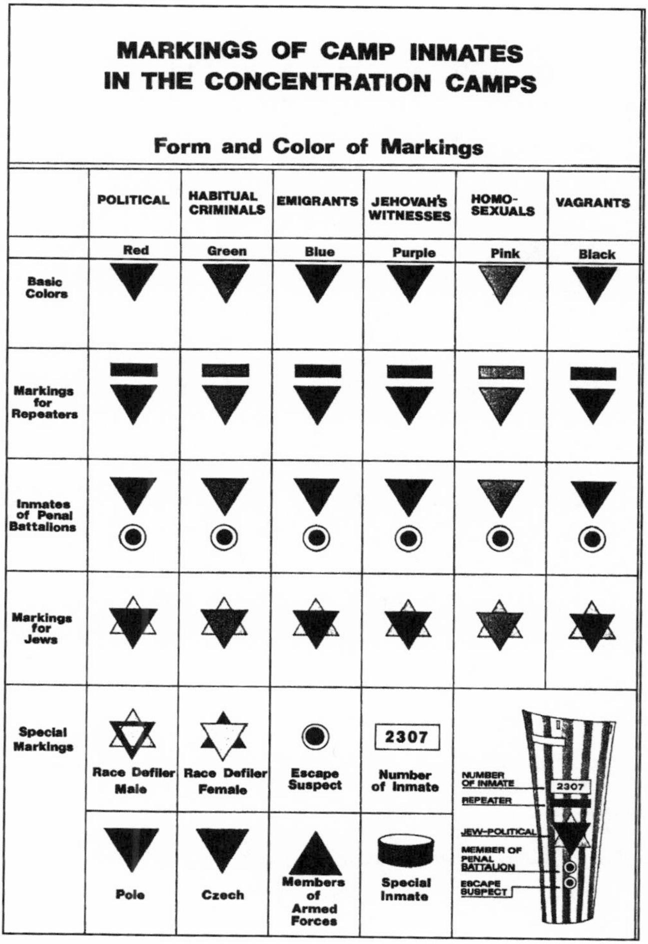

MARKINGS OF CAMP INMATES IN THE CONCENTRATION CAMPS

Form and Color of Markings

	POLITICAL	HABITUAL CRIMINALS	EMIGRANTS	JEHOVAH'S WITNESSES	HOMO-SEXUALS	VAGRANTS
	Red	Green	Blue	Purple	Pink	Black
Basic Colors						
Markings for Repeaters						
Inmates of Penal Battalions						
Markings for Jews						
Special Markings	Race Defiler Male	Race Defiler Female	Escape Suspect	2307 Number of Inmate		
	Pole	Czech	Members of Armed Forces	Special Inmate		

NUMBER OF INMATE
2307
REPEATER
JEW-POLITICAL
MEMBER OF PENAL BATTALION
ESCAPE SUSPECT

Figure 1

Figure 2. "Why is Reagan silent about AIDS? What is really going on at the Center[s] for Disease Control, the Federal Drug Administration, and the Vatican? Gays and lesbians are not expendable . . . Use your power . . . Vote . . . Boycott . . . Defend yourselves . . . Turn anger, fear, grief into action."

also transforms sexuality as a technology of government in a threefold way.

First, lesbians and gay men have, through the invention of relationship techniques and an institutional framework, made it possible to have "sexual freedom" and "true love" at the same time. Because gay and lesbian sexuality can be a celebration of the erotic for its own sake (without the erotic teleology of heterosexism), one can "have sex" with whomever one chooses without, for example, it necessarily impinging upon one's relationship with one's lover, if one chooses to have such a relationship. While this situation is more obvious for gay men, who have more specifically sexual institutions at their disposal, the logic of Hoagland's argument about defragmenting lesbian erotic desire has the same consequences to the extent it reflects or is manifest in the lived experience of lesbians. Lesbian and gay erotics, therefore, can give rise to a variety, in kind and in intensity, of individually modulated relationships, *erotic friendships.* In such friendships, sexuality is a given (neither ruled out nor demanded), and it provides a source for lesbian and gay politics. Indeed, it is the imperative to allow for a rich relational world, "our circle of intimates and their circles and so on,"[17] so that the self can be created within and through it (by casual sex, sex with "intimates," sex within a "couple" relationship, etc.), that is a principal source of lesbian and gay politics.

Second, lesbian and gay erotics transforms how sexuality has historically come to enforce or encourage an inequality between partners, whether con-

17. Hoagland, *Lesbian Ethics*, 174.

ceived as active/passive, top/bottom, or masculine/feminine roles. Lesbian and gay erotics, as I have pointed out, consists in *chosen affinities*. Because they are chosen, they can be un-chosen—what holds the relationship together is the pleasure that the partners give each other. This results in an erotics that integrates the pleasure of the other into one's own pleasure, an ethic of erotic reciprocity. As such, it is the creation of equality within and by means of sexual relationships. This can lead toward social equality (as it has to some degree with lesbian and gay communities—that is not to say there is no class, racial or ethnic, and age stratification there, merely that erotics offers a bridge across these divisions); it also suggests an erotic ethic that can be adapted to male-female sexual relationships as well.

Third, the technology of sexuality creates a fictive unity of the biological (sex) and the historical (gender) that "heterosexualizes" identity in sex-gender (and reproductive) complementarity. Lesbian and gay sexuality takes this unity apart and replaces it with stylization of both biological and historical elements on behalf of erotic pleasure that is also a creation of oneself *as* a self, as an agent in relation with others. (It is in this sense that lesbians and gay men can become "queer," as compared, even in "passing," with people who are not gay or lesbian in their self-presentation in everyday life.) Indeed, as feminism analytically delinked sex from gender in order to demonstrate the potential equality of women with men, the contemporary lesbian and gay movement, to the extent that it incorporates bisexuals and transgendered people, de-essentializes the sexual binary (male/female) itself, the "keeper" of heterosexuality. "Lesbian" and "gay" as political identities arise from ethics, from creating oneself through one's relation to one's own body in relations of sexuality. But lesbians and gays also build upon the already distinct "sex" and "gender" by stylizing each into a *praxis,* what I call erotics. Both sexual anatomy and gender identity are relativized as a foundation for erotic relations and the creation of the self. Such a lesbian and gay ethico-politics may announce a historical transformation in what I have termed the ethical substance we call "sexuality," toward one not referenced to heterosexuality.[18]

Lesbian and gay erotics tends to accomplish the inverse of Catharine MacKinnon's view that "sexuality appears as the interactive dynamic of gender as an inequality. . . . Gender emerges as the congealed form of the sexualization of inequality between men and women." Lesbian erotics can break with the gender subordination involved in heterosexual eroticism and with its reproduction through heterosexual desire. As Judith Butler suggests, gender is constituted through "performativity": performances that cite authoritative sources that, *in their performance,* iterate that authority. Through the refusal of that performance in "coming out" *and* to the extent that performativity is interrupted

18. The concept "sexual praxis" is employed, in a somewhat different fashion, by Robert A. Padgug, "Sexual Matters: On Conceptualizing Sexuality in History," *Radical History Review,* no. 20 (Spring–Summer 1979), 11–18. My point about sexual freedom through this praxis is that it allows the decision to be single or part of a couple or "menage," to be monogamous or engage in casual sexual activity, for example, to be truly an individual choice, rather than coerced through the norms of heterosexism.

through lesbian erotics, essential psychic femininity can be "deprogrammed" from the technology of sexuality, and the normalizing-disciplinary practices of that technology—the prior authoritative set of practices that were cited by the performance of gender—are resisted by lesbians on an individual interpersonal level and, then, collectively on a political level.[19]

By comparison, and in parallel fashion, gay men are in the paradoxical situation of erotically desiring the signs and symbols of masculinity while at the same time undermining it.[20] Masculinity derives its meaning from its relationship of superiority to femininity, incarnated and subjectively iterated in heterosexual sexuality. Male homoerotics eroticizes masculinity; this gay male eroticization of gender equality ("man to man") at the same time undermines manhood to the extent that it is defined through the eroticization of gender inequality in the subordination of women. It is at once being a man and desiring other men, and refusing to be a man as defined through heterosexuality and the subordination of women. In this context, and as a result, we can turn to the words of lesbian feminist Marilyn Frye: "To the extent that gay male culture cultivates and explores and expands its tendencies to the pursuit of simple bodily pleasure . . . it could nurture very radical, hitherto un-

---

19. Catharine A. MacKinnon, *Feminism Unmodified: Discourses on Life and Law* (Cambridge, Mass.: Harvard University Press, 1987), 6; Judith Butler, *Bodies that Matter: On the Discursive Limits of "Sex"* (New York and London: Routledge, 1993). The publication of Butler's book after mine was already completed makes my detailed commenting on it impossible here. The discussion of "performativity" is in chap. 5, "Critically Queer."

20. Pronger, "The Arena of Masculinity," 75.

thinkable new conceptions of what it can be to live as a male body."[21] The habitual practice of homoerotics ("living as a gay man," "living as a lesbian")—what Butler might call subversive repetition—displaces sex/gender as an inequality,[22] since a principal experience that has hitherto produced it within and iterates it through individual subjectivity, sexuality, can cease to do so any longer.

To be sure, equality is central to homoerotic desire. It involves, for lesbians, the desire to employ their erotics to create with and through each other the possibility of agency that is not defined by someone else (as, historically, in the man/woman couple, where the man dominates).[23] For gay men, same-gender erotics involves the desire for gender equality in masculinity, while transforming what masculinity means, to the extent that it is constituted through the subordination of women in heterosexuality. (Gay male drag, for example, mocks heterosexist femininity while ironically imitating it to express one's desire for a man.) However, although homoerotics works through sex/gender, it does not necessarily abolish it on behalf of androgyny but renders it transparent—it de-essentializes it.

---

21. Marilyn Frye, *The Politics of Reality* (Freedom, Calif.: Crossing Press, 1983), 148. In the section from which this passage is drawn, she argues that gay men invent themselves differently from the sexist masculinity of nongay men.

22. I write "sex/gender," following Eve Kosofsky Sedgwick, to denote "the whole package of physical and cultural distinctions between women and men" because, although analytically separable, under the regime of compulsory heterosexuality they are not *enacted* as such except through lesbian, gay, "perverse," queer (nonreproductively—or gender—derived non"sexual") sexualities. This is why I use the term "erotics." Eve Kosofsky Sedgwick, *Epistemology of the Closet* (Berkeley and Los Angeles: University of California Press), 129.

23. For a discussion of this creation of lesbian agency, see Hoagland, *Lesbian Ethics*, especially 6–7.

Lesbians and gay men have joined together in a social-political movement to defend themselves from outright attack and to create a political order that can allow the relational possibilities they have discovered through their sexuality to unfold and be realized. In order for this movement to be effective, social relations of equality between lesbians and gay men have had to become a priority to be realized. (To be sure, political expedience can override the cultivation of friendship between them, and a joint movement has been a historical and strategic imperative.) However, because such an identity politics ultimately relies upon an aesthetic claim for its validity (the goal of erotics is ethical self-constitution as a stylization of one's existence resulting in a shared ethos among lesbians and gay men), the objects of lesbian and gay politics are the norms that inhibit or facilitate such ethical self-constitution. As such, lesbian and gay politics involves a strategy that deploys and calls for legal rights. But its activism is broader than a movement for rights to privacy, equality, and equity alone (as I shall demonstrate). It implies a cultural politics directed at the social conditions underlying regulative norms, as well as at the disciplinary mechanisms of power through which norms are inculcated upon individual bodies and, through them, upon individuals' relations with each other; new ethics, a new relational ethos, would result in new cultural forms.

Chapter 4

What Are Lesbian and Gay Rights?

Sexual intimacy is a sensitive, key relationship of human existence. . . . The fact that individuals define themselves in a significant way through their intimate sexual relationships . . . touches the heart of what makes individuals what they are.

Justice Harry A. Blackmun, dissenting in *Bowers v. Hardwick*

[Everyone has] the right to establish and to develop relationships with other human beings, especially in the emotional field for the development and fulfillment of one's own personality.

European Commission on Human Rights

The notion of "lesbian and gay rights" has come to mean the relationship of lesbians and gay men to the state. It has meant limiting the state's power with respect to them as persons, as well as what the state should, in a positive sense, do to aid such individuals in the satisfaction of their basic needs. This relationship has become a political issue on three levels. First, the lesbian and gay movement has striven for the abolition of laws that restrict or prohibit sexual relations between consenting partners, the right to be left alone by the state. Second, it has striven for the right to equal protection of the laws and against discrimination in housing, employment, and public accommodation for people who choose others of the same sex as sexual partners. Following from this demand for equal treatment, the movement has asserted the subsidiary right to have the relationships that may develop out of one's sexual expression recognized legally, institutionally, and socially. This would confer upon them the same advantages as those held by the only sexual-affectional relations that are currently recognized, those of marriage and biological family. (Such legal and institutional recognition has been articulated, for example, in the demand for the legalization of gay/lesbian marriage, in proposals for domestic-partnership legislation, and, analogously, in judicial decisions that recognize the diversity of affective—"family"—relationships.) Finally, the movement has asserted the right to distributive justice in the administration of the benefits of citizenship through the satisfaction of those needs that are fundamental to self-determination and self-actualization—in particular, the means to sexual health.

Sexuality and Normativity: A Relational Right

I conceptualize here within rights discourse: the significance of sexuality in living our lives today—of erotic (sexual-affectional) relations in the cultivation of the self; social and legal recognition of this significance (which is already at least tacit for heterosexual relations); and a claim upon society's resources based upon this significance in order to foster such relations. To do so I expand beyond the previous formulation of "lesbian and gay rights," derived mainly from sexual privacy, that tends to put gays and lesbians on the defensive as an interest group expressing a subjective preference and move toward a formulation that affirms lesbian and gay existence with broader cultural underpinnings. Drawing on early gay liberation language, which speaks of "our right to love," I call it a "relational right."[1] This right would therefore incorporate the three "moments" in the contemporary struggle for lesbian and gay rights: for sexual freedom, for equality, and for equity. While the assertion of such a right may make use of legal strategies of "privacy" for consensual sexual expression, of equal protection for nondiscrimination, and of distributive justice for recognition to receive the benefits of citizenship, it goes beyond a juridico-discursive model of rights as granted to or withheld from individuals by the *state* to a conceptualization of a right within a normalizing-disciplinary ordering of power. Such a right would

1. The specific formulation "relational right" was, I believe, first put into print in a conversation between Gilles Barbedette and Michel Foucault and in 1982. It has become a stock phrase, however, among lesbians and gay men when referring to new forms of relationships that deserve social recognition and legal legitimation. Michel Foucault, "The Social Triumph of the Sexual Will: A Conversation with Michel Foucault," *Christopher Street*, no. 64 (1982): 36–41. The formulation there is very schematic; see also Kath Weston, *Families We Choose: Lesbians, Gays, Kinship* ((New York: Columbia University Press, 19, 1991); *The Family Relationships Project of Lambda Legal Defense and Education Fund* (New York: Lambda Legal Defense and Education Fund, 1990); and Suzanne Sherman, ed., *Lesbian and Gay Marriage: Private Commitments, Public Ceremonies* (Philadelphia: Temple University Press, 1992).

employ legal codification, but its principal mode of expression would be with respect to the normalizing-disciplinary relations of power that are often camouflaged by the juridical model. The relational right is pressed, via "coming out" as lesbian or gay, to change the normalizing-disciplinary practices of compulsory heterosexuality in everyday life, but both in order to do so and as a consequence, its assertion has recourse to the legal system.

The "privacy strategy" for lesbian and gay rights is necessary but has its limits. One principal legal problem facing the lesbian and gay movement has been the criminalization of sexual activity between persons of the same sex (through, in the United States, for example, sodomy laws and the discriminatory application of sexual-solicitation and public-lewdness statutes). This not only has a preemptive effect, by providing the lock on the closet door for many lesbian and gay people, but it also has the real force of imprisonment, fines, trials, and police harassment that large numbers of lesbian and gay citizens have endured.[2]

---

2. Aggregate data on the number of arrests for sexual solicitation and sodomy apparently do not exist on the state or national levels in the United States, according to Sue Hyde, director of the Privacy Project of the National Gay and Lesbian Task Force (the project works for the repeal of all U.S. state sodomy laws). In an interview with me on March 13, 1990, she stated that to get such data one would have to tally the arrest statistics of the district attorneys of every country in the United States.

A fairly typical example of the use of such laws, which received public attention in 1990, involved the Vince Lombardi Memorial Rest Stop on the New Jersey Turnpike. In 1989, plainclothes officers made 540 arrests of men there on "lewdness" charges, netting the local authorities more than $200,000 in fines. (In New Jersey statutes, a lewd act "shall include the exposing of the genitals for the purpose of arousing or gratifying the sexual desire of the actor or of another person.") According to attorneys (as reported by *The Advocate*), "undercover officers made most of their arrests by flirting with unaccompanied men

While one could argue that sodomy laws should be abolished because they unjustly regulate everyone's sexual expression, in fact "liberalization" by the U.S. states has often meant permitting a greater variety of heterosexual acts while still prohibiting homosexual ones. The United States Supreme Court, in *Bowers v. Hardwick* (1986), even affirmed the states' rights to legislate against homosexual, as distinct from heterosexual, sodomy. Lesbians and gay men find, therefore, that not only are they denied equal protection under the laws, not only can their sexual choices place them in prison for up to twenty years, but also that any "predisposition" to have a sexual relationship can result in, if not imprisonment, then devastating personal, social, and economic consequences (and often does—unlike sodomy laws, which are difficult to enforce, solicitation and lewdness laws *are* enforced, almost always through entrapment).[3] Sodomy and solicitation

---

at the rest stop and pretending to masturbate at urinals. . . . 'Police set up a sexual atmosphere [and,] in many cases, nobody was even having sex. Even some straight people were arrested.' " Between January 1988 and October 1989, only 15 of the 370 cases heard by the municipal judge resulted in dismissals or not-guilty verdicts. This points out not only the state's economic interest in policing sexuality but also the inhibiting effect on the victims in challenging such blatant entrapment—because of the "embarrassment and possibility of discrimination that follow such charges," most men pleaded guilty. See Chris Bull, "N.J. Cops Say They Will Keep Their Pants On," *The Advocate*, no. 547 (March 27, 1990): 18.

In addition to direct enforcement, sodomy laws can be used to hinder AIDS prevention and sex education generally, to justify housing discrimination, and to discriminate against lesbians and gays in child custody and visitation proceedings, for example—all through criminalizing lesbian and gay sexual relations.

3. According to Richard Mohr: "The content of sodomy laws has varied widely from time to time, state to state, and country to country. Laws have ranged from barring only anal penetrations of males by males to barring all permutations of contacts between mouth, genitals,

laws are basic to contemporary lesbian and gay existence since they codify domination and thereby support the most extreme form of subjection, the social invisibility (as a consequence of being "in the closet") of lesbian and gay people.

The much-vaunted "right to privacy" does not fully work as a restorative. Although the assertion of such a right by the movement has been useful in convincing nongays to decriminalize homosexual expression, and even to support equal-treatment and nondiscrimination laws (since homosexuality, it is argued, is irrelevant in job performance, housing, and public accommodations and therefore is an improper area of inquiry), such a strategy *alone* can exacerbate the oppression of gay people. What is least tolerated about homosexuality is not the sex acts themselves (since they are rarely engaged in "in public view" anyway), but the *appearance*, the social visibility of lesbian and gay people and their affectional relations with each

---

and anus except kissing and genital contacts between those married to each other." Thus, Texas's "liberal" sodomy statute permits "oral and anal sex among heterosexual couples, but not among gay and lesbian couples," and Mississippi's is one of the broadest and most restrictive: "Every person who shall be convicted of the detestable crime against nature, committed with mankind or with beast, shall be punished by imprisonment in the penitentiary for a term of not more than ten years." In 1989, twenty-four states had sodomy statutes, with punishments of up to twenty years in prison. Mohr argues from legal principle for the abolition of solicitation and lewdness laws. These laws also reflect a paranoid rationalization that undergirds the "homosexual panic" or "gay advance" defense in antigay violent crimes: "defendants claim self-defense or temporary insanity in response to a sexual advance to win lenient sentences or acquittals when charged with assaulting or murdering gay men." Richard R. Mohr, *Gays/Justice: A Study of Ethics, Society, and Law* (New York: Columbia University Press, 1988), 51, 54–55, and particularly his excellent chap. 2, "Why Sodomy Laws Are Bad."See also Peter Freiberg, "New Report on Hate Crimes," *The Advocate*, no. 488 (December 22, 1987): 10–11, 20.

other throughout the fabric of social life—in the sense of social acknowledgment of one's identity as being gay or lesbian, and any open display of affection that might be construed by others as homoerotic, as distinct from "just friendly." The privacy strategy leaves what I referred to as the "heterosexual panorama" intact; it elides it as a normalizing-disciplinary ordering of power. Indeed it is, following Butler, the *performing* of gay and lesbian relationships that interrupts the disciplining of power while invoking different relational norms.

Rather than being conceived merely as a right to privacy, which is usually conceived as a right to one's (homoerotic) affections as long as they are kept hidden socially, lesbian and gay rights need to be conceptualized following the model of "coming out"—but as more than mere individual self-revelation. The model should involve a right to self-determination of one's relationships with others that is asserted against and through disciplinary practices that constitute heterosexuality as normative.[4]

---

4. The social and legal implications of coming out also need to be addressed. According to a study commissioned by the U.S. Department of Justice, "the visibility of gay men" is a possible reason for the increase in bias crimes (especially personal attacks, as distinct from vandalism) against gay men and lesbians. The study also found that "homosexuals are probably the most frequent victims of hate-motivated violence and are targeted for assault, verbal intimidation, and vandalism more often than Blacks, Hispanics, Southeast Asians, and Jews." It concludes that "the vast majority of police departments and district attorneys' offices around the country have failed to address the problem of hate-motivated violence [and] that excluding homosexuals from protection under bias crime legislation—as has occurred in many states—either condones bias crimes against gays and lesbians or suggests it does not exist" (cited in Freiberg, "New Report on Hate Crimes," 10). Furthermore, the National Gay and Lesbian Task Force cites an annual increase in *reported* incidents of slayings, assaults, threats, and verbal harassment against gay people: 7,248 in 1988 (in-

Although norms are merely the principles of comparability and standards of reference within a society by means of which individuals become intelligible as such, they are created through procedures of observation and surveillance of individuals that, statistically or otherwise, allow for knowledge about an average which then enables development of social policy based upon it (that includes fostering the "normal" and disallowing, or sanctioning with the aim of making performative within the norm, the "abnormal"). The "appearance" of a heterosexual human essence is only that; what appears through individual self-examination and verbalization to authorities surveilling the population can be the product of a power relationship through which an individual relates himself or herself to the "average" that has been produced through such procedures of data collection; and, it can be endemic to the collection process itself—possibilities other than heterosexuality are not looked for or disguised within it (as when men who have sex with men do not exist because they do not identify as "gay"). This knowledge then serves as a basis for governmental policies and society's reflection upon itself through, say, the mass media, the census, opinion

---

cluding 70 slayings), 7,008 in 1987, 4,946 in 1986, and 2,042 in 1985 an increase that has been confirmed by other organizations that monitor bias-related violence. See Philip S. Gutis, "Attacks on U.S. Homosexuals Held Alarmingly Widespread," *New York Times*, June 8, 1989, A24. According to the director of the NGLTF's Anti-Violence Project, there was a 128 percent increase from 1988 to 1993. The visibility of lesbians also provokes violence against them. In a 1989 case in Pennsylvania, where one member of a lesbian couple was murdered and the other was wounded, the defense asserted that the defendant was provoked by seeing their physical affection toward each other after he had followed them to a secluded campground.

surveys, and so on, reinforcing heterosexuality as normative. Since what counts as an individual is constituted through society's procedures for establishing standards of comparability and communication *among* individuals, then individuality itself is purely relational. A relational right therefore involves a claim to individuate oneself through relationships, to receive recognition through those procedures establishing standards of comparison by means of which individuals are "counted," and to expand those standards. Changing sexual normativity from compulsory heterosexuality—changing the boundary between the normal (heterosexuality) and abnormal (homosexuality)—means making relations whose existence and possibilities were already inherent in social life "recognized" by those procedures through which we, as a society, observe and measure ourselves and develop policies accordingly to govern ourselves (as the 1990 U.S. census enabled counting same-sex households). Hence the centrality of "coming out" and lesbian and gay "visibility."

The meaning of lesbian and gay rights must therefore be conceptualized in relation to how these norms regarding sexuality get established, how they get grounded in truth claims and what kinds of truth those claims claim, and their power effects, say, for the generational transmission of capital and social structure, and for how sexual relationships are objectified as a factor in education and public health policy. Lesbians and gays, through the erotic relationships by means of which they individuate or *create* themselves, make a claim upon *normativity*—the common standards of measurement, evaluation, and comparability through which individual difference becomes intelligible among members of society—how we come to know ourselves through society's reflection upon itself—and how these standards come into being. They make this claim upon normativity without regard to "human nature" (i.e., sex-gender-reproductive complementarity that flows from and iterates the privileging of heterosexuality) but rather according to a principle that might be formulated as an open question: "What relationships shall we have and how shall we make up the rules for them?"

Since erotics is a principal way through which lesbians and gay men constitute themselves as agents of their own actions in relations with others, any legal restrictions on sexual choice—when one consensually enters into a sexual relationship and understands any medical risks involved—would prevent self-determination and actualization. A right to privacy (supposedly justified because sexual expression is inherently "world excluding," since it is "conducted out of the sensory range of nonparticipants [and] ought clearly to invoke substantive immunities from government intrusions")[5] can focus only upon the *state's* regulation of sexual *acts*. It elides the power relations that constitute compulsory heterosexuality, and it is not adequate conceptually to deal with the other components of the "gay rights" legal agenda, nondiscrimination and equity. Thus, a better way to conceptualize the normative agenda of the lesbian and gay movement is through a *relational* right.

---

5. Mohr, *Gays/Justice*, 125.

A way to formulate such a right is to locate its source in the *meaning* that a relationship has for the individuals involved in it. Thus, erotic choice can only be intelligible to others by taking into account the meaning of that choice for the individual (to maximize a bodily sensation or to achieve personal autonomy, for example), that is, its value in self-constitution. Such a "hermeneutic" understanding of a right locates it in the ethical experience of lesbians and gay men;[6] provides a basis for conceiving how erotics is relational (i.e., that it is the mutual creation of agency by individuals, to be sure, within the context of social power relations, but within which erotics presupposes reciprocity); and, finally, provides a rationale for a claim for rights that, although they use the state as a resource, are ultimately directed toward the normalizing-disciplinary exercise of power that constitutes sexuality as compulsory heterosexuality.

The source of a relational right, then, resides in individuals' need for relational freedom—the freedom to choose their sexual-affectional relations with others—in order to constitute themselves as ethical beings. In such erotic relationships, to the extent that they are *chosen* by the individual (consented to), peoples' actions become conditions for the becoming of each other. A relational right, however, raises the problem of what constitutes freedom of individual

6. By "hermeneutic," I mean the analysis of the *self-understanding* of participants involved in a cultural practice (such as an erotic relationship) in terms of how that self-understanding is shaped by language and the power relations within which that practice takes place, in order to understand the cultural practice. For an analogous understanding of rights, see Patricia J. Williams, *The Alchemy of Race and Rights* (Cambridge, Mass.: Harvard University Press, 1991), especially 104–10.

choice in such relations, what is often called (in the legal vocabulary) "informed consent." Indeed, since a relational right, strictly speaking, concerns not primarily relations of commercial transaction (a right to contract with others) or freedom of association (the right to form groups with others) but, rather, sexual-affectional relations (relations of bodily and emotional pleasure through which participants develop selfhood), in seeking the source of a relational right one must analyze what "informed consent" to, a *choice* of, "pleasure" means.

Experiencing pleasure encompasses more than bodily pleasure, and even bodily pleasure is more than sexual or genital pleasure. Nevertheless, a relational right concerns the relations that people have through which, by the use of their bodies, they give each other pleasure. The starting point for analyzing the experience of pleasure among lesbians and gay men is through their erotics—sexuality as ethical substance, sources of authority for its use, sexual practices or techniques, and its purposes or outcomes—as discussed in Chapter 3. According to the lesbian theorist Cindy Patton, pleasures are

> sensual perceptions or interactions which when assigned to categories begin to create zones on the body. When pleasures and their corresponding body zones are given social meaning and value, there emerges a self-consciousness about the body; . . . the recognition of these body zones with their attendant pleasures, and the evaluation of these zones and pleasures, invite the choice to pursue particular acts that will recognize the zones and pleasures. . . . The subject's possibility of willing [as the method of attaining

> particular pleasures] creates a sense of agency—a sense of being able to unite pleasures and acts in a system consonant with the subject's organization of the zones. But, of course, all zones are not equal, and they are arbitrary to begin with. . . . Although the idea of sexual pleasure may be universal in some form, the permissible acts for attaining that pleasure, as well as the exact content and extent of the zones designated as sexual, are still governed by laws of language, and supported by religious and legal mechanisms.
>
> Subjectivity is constructed by the possibility of agency in directing those pleasures [not merely] the pursuit of pleasure and the avoidance of pain—for the very categories of experience identified as pleasure or pain have undergone extensive definition before they are projected as possible outcomes of [sexual agency].[7]

Thus, what pleasure means is historically defined, and the actions of a subject to attain sexual pleasure must be interpreted through the cultural organization (hierarchization, prohibition, existence as such) of both the zones of the body that can give pleasure as well as the means for attaining it. As noted in Chapter 3, what pleasure *can be* undergoes continuous definition and redefinition through the mode of subjection of lesbians and gay men (the lesbian and gay community). This community serves as a means of communication and of education, interacting with members' subjectivities within the actual ethico-erotic practices

7. Cindy Patton, *Sex and Germs: The Politics of AIDS* (Boston: South End Press, 1985), 117.

through which they act upon each other's bodies to produce pleasure.

In order to interpret, then, the meaningfulness of relationships to their participants, one has to take into account this relativity of what pleasure means. One must consider how individuals understand themselves as actualizing themselves, creating themselves as agents, as subjects of their actions through such relationships that vary in kind and in intensity. It is here that the context of the relationship is significant. Of course, a sexual-affectional relationship always takes place in the context of other social relationships and in the context of power that is exercised through them, whether this power be gender- or race- or class-based, for example. However, the basis for a relational right is the expressed reciprocal exercise of agency by individuals party to the relationship. In interpreting normatively erotic relations, one can examine: Are the erotic practices in the relationship *chosen* by the partners or was a partner coerced? How safe are the practices, and are the participants informed of any risks involved? What do *partners* say is happening in an erotic "scene"; for example, in one involving role-playing, is there reciprocity? What is the difference between the infliction of erotic pain and assault?

One way of hermeneutically interpreting and evaluating what happens in an erotic relationship is through the rubric "safe, sane, and consensual." (This rubic is becoming current within gay and lesbian discourse about sexuality as absorbed from the discourse of "ideal typical" erotic situations such as safer sex workshops and S/M, as well as from community-based programs aimed at domestic violence prevention.) First, a sexual relation must not inflict irreversible harm on the participants (e.g., permanent physical disability or infection with a sexually transmitted disease). Also, "safety" is not absolute: there are degrees of risk in activities that involve the body, and thus another principle, consent, implies deliberation and communication among the participants about what degree of risk is acceptable for particular activities (e.g., piercing or the exchange of bodily fluids). Consent must be ongoing: one does not consent once and for all, either in an erotic scene or to participate in a continuous relationship (e.g., to be someone's slave, thereby giving the other permanent power over one even within specified limits). There must be the opportunity for each party in the relationship to review and revise to what it is they are consenting. In an S/M scene, for example, the parties use "safe words" like "yellow" (approaching limit) or "red" (limit of consent) to regulate the relationship. Similarly, there need to be ways of regulating ongoing relationships through consultation with external parties; indeed, this would be establishing different relationality (with other friends, with a therapist, through social networks) to ensure the continuing nature of consent, thus monitoring normativity. The necessity for ongoing consent is, finally, exemplified in the fact that one cannot "consent" to be permanently dominated or killed by another (whether in an erotic scene or not), since there would then be no more possibility for consent. (Euthanasia, a separate but related topic, constitutes an exception. If it is agreed in advance that when consent can no longer be given, and when life has ceased to be "sane" according to previously agreed upon criteria of quality of life, then life can be taken, as embodied in a living will.)

Consent will also provide a basis for determining when governmental agencies may intervene in people's erotic relations with each other. This brings up the third aspect of erotic normativity, "sanity." As Cindy Patton suggests, what pleasure consists in is culturally and historically constructed, but there is also great room for individual variation: one person's pain is another person's pleasure, and vice versa. Although lack of consent can turn erotic actions into assault or rape, since erotics is a *formation* of the self it implies a claim by the individual upon normativity itself, how individuals become "individual," based solely upon their adaptation to society. Ultimately, what is "sane" in erotic life is defined by the *limits* one establishes for *oneself* relationally—sexuality conceived aesthetically. (One's preferences, sexual and more generally relational, could be unintelligible, "not my cup of tea," or incompatible with limits expressed by life choices, for others.) In an erotic relationship, one must articulate those limits to one's partner or other participants, and they must be respected or the consensuality of the relationship is violated. As such, "sanity," the setting of limits for oneself by oneself, is exemplary of the intelligibility and further constitution of selfhood within erotic relationships and, as interdependent with safety and consent, is a framework for normatively interpreting those relationships.

Gay and lesbian erotics makes visible the structural constraints on sexual choice embedded in the social order as compulsory heterosexuality. It is through erotics that lesbians and gay men subjectively confront these constraints and then make claims for their transformation on the basis of gay rights as a relational right. (Erotics, again, includes all the self-shaping sexual practices discussed in Chapter 3, but here also the erotic culture created by those practices, including open discussion within the forums and media of the lesbian and gay community *about* sexual choices.) This is a right to erotico-aesthetic *choice* subject to interpretation and evaluation by others according to criteria of *self-creation* (say, whether choices are safe, sane, and manifest consent as defined here) rather than to criteria based upon recourse to "truth" derived from statistical or other conceptualizations of normality (even though it may come to have an effect upon these latter conceptualizations).

Thus, there are two aspects to consider in conceiving lesbian and gay rights in a broader cultural context as a relational right. First, the right to have the kinds of erotic relationships one chooses is not only exercised vis-à-vis "the state" as such but, rather, vis-à-vis all the institutions that set frameworks for the kinds of relationships it is possible to have in our society. We are governed not only by the state's laws but by kinship, medical, economic, professional, religious, recreational, and other institutions. It is these institutions that prescribe forms of conduct based upon certain rationales in order for individuals to participate in and receive benefits from them. It is both to the way these relate to more comprehensive regulatory rationales and capacities that include legal ones and to how, through them, power is exercised on the "capillary" level, *as they constitute a technology of government—*

that shapes our possible sexual-affectional relations with each other—that they thus provide a target for rights. (This is also demonstrated in the political theory of the rights of employees, students, patients, adoptive parents, and cultural minorities, for example. See notes 9 and 28.) Therefore, the assertion of a relational right shifts the balance of power away from the state as the sole guarantor of rights belonging to a *juridical* subject toward a plurality of sites for the recognition of rights. The existence of gay and lesbian *relationships* throughout the institutional framework of society, as well as the coming out of individuals, undermines domination—compulsory heterosexuality—and opens up sexual normativity to a greater range of human possibilities.

Second, the source of the right is a relational subject-in-the-making. (This is not to say that a conception of "universal human rights" should be abandoned as a baseline for formulating relational rights.) A relational right derives from the fact that the individual "becomes" through relationships—for example, one may be heterosexual and bear children in one relationship and become homosexual in another. Similarly, bisexuals do not want to be punished for being categorized as "homosexual" in one context and "heterosexual" in another—they claim a right to *choose* their own sexual relationships. Hence, the relational right derives from what it means to be truly individual. It consists in a claim of individuality—of the right to choose the kinds of relationships that allow one to fulfill oneself, "become," be "happy," and so on—within a (normalizing-disciplinary) ordering of power that operates by defining the identity of individuals (according to the "normal" and deviations from it) and shapes individual choices (through relational rewards, punishments, or nonrecognition) to approximate the norm, that is, discipline. Individual behavior is at once the object on the basis of which norms emerge and the instruments through which they are enforced. Within this context, individuals claim the right to invent their own standards of happiness and, through making this intelligible in their relationships with others, have them accepted as "normal"—as within the range of human possibility. In this way, normativity need not so much be conceived as a matter of constraints imposed on individuals as, again, the common standards for comparison and communication through which we make ourselves intelligible to each other. As such a principle of mutual intelligibility, norms and the normative can be totally devoid of metaphysical meaning and independent of religious or philosophic conviction.

Lesbian and gay rights, therefore, need not be conceived as a revolutionary challenge to society and their assertion need not wait for some future time when society will be more "tolerant." As expressing a right to love whom one chooses in a way mutually acceptable, such a relational right finds its support from and applications far beyond lesbian and gay existence. The aim of this right, in the language of the Los Angeles Task Force on Family Diversity, is "to strengthen the freely chosen affectional relationships that individuals have with each other."[8] Although the movement has used a "rights strategy" of civil liberty and equal treatment for basic legal protection (see the "Demands" of the 1993 March on Washington, for example, reproduced in the conclusion of this chapter), this is only a first step. The relational right is really formulated with respect to and expressed through the normalizing-disciplinary practices by means of which power is exercised in contemporary everyday life. While coming out breaks through the discipline of the heterosexual panorama, the relational right of same-sex erotic affection challenges the normativity of compulsory heterosexuality. Since it is through sexuality that the modern self is to a large extent both created and governed, it is the lesbian, gay, bisexual, and transgender movement that is the historical medium through which a politics of sexuality yields a relational right that benefits all.

There is, however, another aspect of the lesbian and gay movement's assertion of rights: equity. In the context of modern biopower, rights also come from the fact that we are living beings with needs that must be

---

8. Remarks of Christopher McCauley, cochair of the Los Angeles Task Force on Family Diversity, before the Association of the Bar of the City of New York, January 12, 1989. See also *Strengthening Families: A Model for Community Action*, Final Report to the City of Los Angeles by the Task Force on Family Diversity, May 19, 1988. Some of the most suggestive conceptualizations for analyzing the assertion of rights toward nonstate organizations of power are in David W. Ewing, *Freedom Inside the Organization: Bringing Civil Liberties to the Workplace* (New York: McGraw-Hill, 1977); Williams, *Alchemy of Race and Rights*; Chandran Kukathas, "Are There Any Cultural Rights?" *Political Theory* 20(1) (February 1992): 105–39; *The ACLU "Rights of" Series*, American Civil Liberties Union, 132 West 43 St., New York, NY 10036, 1971–present; and William B. Rubenstein, ed., *Lesbians, Gay Men, and the Law* (New York: The New Press, 1993).

satisfied, and the technology of sexuality has made us living beings with sexual needs that are satisfied relationally. Modern government is concerned with managing the life process—both to protect populations from themselves and to protect individuals from the risks that others expose them to, as well as allowing populations and individuals to realize their potentials. Life is a wealth that must be tapped; as U.S. President Clinton said in decrying discrimination against lesbians and gays, "We don't have a person to waste." Within such a context, lesbian and gay rights get formulated also on behalf of a *need* for sexual health, and a right of access to protection from any biological risks derived from sexual relations. As with the other "moments" of lesbian and gay rights, the movement for the right to "safe sex" has followed a juridical "rights strategy." This involves a demand that public health include sexual health—in particular, that the state fund research for treatments and a cure for AIDS (as well as other sexually transmitted diseases) and fund preventive sexual education. However, as AIDS has come to be conceptualized as a chronic disease like cancer or diabetes (what some have even called the "cancerization" of AIDS), the right takes on a more significant expression with regard to the normalizing-disciplinary management of life on behalf of medical knowledge, by means of biotechnologies and by doctors and other life specialists who determine whether individuals are sick, and through power exercised by those who can protect the well from the sick and from sickness, maximizing "social health." I turn now to the assertion of lesbian and gay rights through the politicization of AIDS.

Chapter 4

AIDS and Biopower

I have examined how lesbian and gay rights are asserted against the normalizing-disciplinary order of compulsory heterosexuality. This assertion involves a claim for justice, based not upon metaphysical claims but upon procedures by which norms are constituted—upon normativity itself. In this section, I extend the claim for justice to include equity in the cultural and social acknowledgment of one's health needs and the consequent receipt of the benefits of citizenship. Since sexuality is coincidental to lesbian and gay ethical self-constitution, justice consists in the right of access to the *means* of sexual health. This would include the availability of education about sexuality, as well as having protection from biological risks involved in the exercise of one's sexual-relational freedom. Lesbian and gay rights, understood as a right to have the means for health available, would include: access to means of protection from and treatment for sexually transmitted diseases (STDs), including AIDS, and for breast cancer (since its incidence is higher among women who do not conceive children—a population which would disproportionately include lesbians); access to reproductive technology—principally, alternative insemination for lesbians who wish to conceive children; and access to sex-reassignment surgery. All of these have been demands of the U.S. lesbian and gay movement because they follow directly from ethical self-constitution through the use of one's sexuality.

Here, I will analyze the politics of AIDS because it is a principal contemporary example of how the movement has asserted the right to sexual health and because I am a gay man who has been personally affected by and motivated to take political action because of the epidemic. Analyses of specifically lesbian and transgender health needs must inform any assertion of rights by the movement; I hope contemporary AIDS activism can provide insights for such analyses and political assertion.[9] Further, it is difficult to write about AIDS because one's remarks are rapidly outdated by biomedical developments. However, what I try to create in this section is an analytical framework for understanding how AIDS was made a political issue by gay men (and later, through AIDS activism, by lesbians and nongay people), an understanding of the implication of the emergence of AIDS for sexuality as a technology of government, and what lesbian and gay rights mean in the context of the AIDS epidemic.

What has come to be called AIDS has arisen at the point of superimposition of sexuality as a technology of government upon the historically prior one of biological kinship, and the reinscription of the latter within the former. What is striking from a political perspective, besides the number of deaths from this disease and the lack of medical progress in arresting it by the time of this writing, is that AIDS constitutes a *remedicalization* of sexuality. To the extent that the women's and gay/lesbian movements have been historically instrumental in removing sexuality from ways of conceptualizing it that engendered heterosexism and homophobia (based upon religious and then psy-

9. For example, see the annual conference proceedings of the National Lesbian and Gay Health Association, 1407 S Street, N.W., Washington, D.C., 20009.

chiatric modes of reasoning), AIDS has allowed sexuality's translation *from* the discourse of hetero = truth and homo = error *into* a discourse of risk assessment of particular behaviors, and risk management and reduction, thereby undercutting the power authorized by the hetero-homo discourse. However, in spite of this less metaphysical and "kinder and gentler" installation of sexuality into "the truth," the "regime of truth" that has coalesced since the naming of the epidemic in 1981 has been the object of a fierce politicization by gay men and, later, by others.

By "regime" I mean to say that the medicalization of sexuality facilitated through AIDS involves a threefold relationship between knowledge and power. First, the disease syndrome, AIDS, was constructed as a largely sexually transmitted one (sexuality imbricated with knowing and telling the truth about a domain of life, "disease"). Second, this medicalization of sexuality was supported by epidemiological research (what are the affected populations), symptomological decisions (what individual physical manifestations "count" as AIDS), etiological hypotheses (what causes the physical manifestations and death that is AIDS), and by medical experts who could speak the truth about AIDS. Third, the medicalization of sexuality through AIDS enabled certain people to exercise power coercively, such as that wielded by public health officials, or "pastorally"—through subjection—such as that wielded by clinical physicians, therapists, and ministers, for example.

The politics of the medicalization of sexuality through AIDS must be understood in a historical context. Recall that physicians and psychiatrists medicalized homosexuality in the nineteenth century, thereby providing a "scientific" rationale for state intervention, as well as the means for its achievement through declaration of mental disability and then institutionalization. The counterdiscourse of homosexuality among activists and within sexology and psychiatry led the American Psychiatric Association in 1973 to finally remove homosexuality from its list of mental disorders. However, this took place in the context of a long history of the absence of nonjudgmental and preventive intervention with regard to gay male health by the medical establishment. Some gay men received good treatment, but as middle-class men, not as gays.[10] Most gay men were afraid to come out to their doctors because of the latters' moralizing judgments about deserving their ailments due to their "promiscuity" and about the need to treat their "lifestyle" (even though it may take only one encounter to transmit an infectious agent, including the human immunodeficiency virus, or HIV, believed by many at the time of this writing to cause AIDS). Many gays were afraid to come out, as well, because of mandatory reporting to government agencies of sexually transmitted diseases and because of possible public exposure. It was not until the late 1970s that some doctors recognized that the lesbian and gay community might have its health needs better met through treat-

10. See Jeffrey Weeks, *Sex, Politics, and Society: The Regulation of Sexuality since 1800* (London: Longman, 1981), chaps. 6 and 8; Ronald Bayer, *Homosexuality and American Psychiatry: The Politics of Diagnosis* (New York: Basic Books, 1981); Robert Padgug, "More than the Story of a Virus: Gay History, Gay Communities, and AIDS," *Radical America*, 1(2–3): 41.

ment within the context of that community. Even this notion, however, was put forth by the gay community itself and by openly lesbian and gay physicians (most other doctors refused even to acknowledge the existence of such a community, or acknowledged it through a "blaming the victim" prejudice).[11] By then, the history of "mismanagement of the health of the gay community left it particularly vulnerable to new diseases, among which AIDS is not the only example, although it is the most devastating. This same history created a gay community determined to play a significant role in the medical management of AIDS."[12]

Despite this general neglect of lesbian and gay male sexual health historically, however, medical discourse in the late 1970s and early 1980s came to view male homosexuality as medically problematic. This discourse was constituted by reports from clinical and laboratory research appearing in medical journals with citing and cross-referencing on the same thematic content: prior assumptions that *being gay* was

---

11. William W. Darrow, Donald Barrett, Karla Jay, and Allen Young, "The Gay Report on Sexually Transmitted Diseases," *American Journal of Public Health* 71(9) (September 1981): 10004–11. See also the editorial in the same issue by H. Hunter Handsfield, "Sexually Transmitted Diseases in Homosexual Men," which calls for the "education of practicing physicians to non-judgmentally inquire into alternative sexual lifestyles and to recognize and appropriately manage the major STD syndromes." Handsfield argues that the growth of gay STD clinics is "prime facie evidence that the local health department and/or local physicians have failed an important responsibility," and that the continued reliance on such clinics would be counterproductive "because most would not be able to provide the comprehensive services necessary [which *should* be provided by public STD clinics and medical centers] and [would] stigmatize gay men and their unique health problems by removing them from the mainstream of medical care."

12. Padgug, "More than the Story," 41.

possibly an illness in itself, assertions that male homosexual *practices* are inherently unhealthy, and stereotypes of the gay male *lifestyle* as one of overindulgence in sex and drugs that led to an overload of the immune system.[13]

A biological phenomenon, therefore, instigated a remedicalization of gay male sexual practices, sexual identity, and lifestyle that, for the gay community, instigated a viewing as "political," not just neutrally "scientific," of medical knowledge and the exercise of power it authorized. This politicization of medical knowledge and power in the context of the epidemic was at once a defense against medical homophobia and heterosexism and a way in which gay men (and later lesbians) were able to empower themselves as individuals, and their organizations as political actors, to shape the future development of the epidemic. Thus a self-help AIDS-activist movement emerged, comprised of HIV-positive people, people with AIDS, and their friends and advocates. While the organizations they formed and the benefits they reaped have not been exclusively lesbian and gay, the most successful groups have been led overwhelmingly by gay men (later joined by lesbians), and have thus been able to draw upon the resources of the existing organizations of the lesbian and gay movement for their support, both financial and tactical.[14]

---

13. See, also, Steven Epstein, "Moral Contagion and the Medicalizing of Gay Identity: AIDS in Historical Perspective," *Research in Law, Deviance, and Social Control* 9 (1988): 3–36, especially 14–15.

14. For a discussion of the tensions between AIDS activism and the lesbian and gay rights movement generally, see Darrell Yates Rist,

How did the politicization by the lesbian and gay movement of this government through AIDS unfold? There are three elements to consider. First, the movement problematized the definition of the situation it was in:[15] it publicly monitored and criticized medical conceptualization, from deaths supposedly incident to the hazards of gay male sexuality and lifestyle, to a disease of "risk groups" (homosexuals, intravenous drug users, Haitians, hemophiliacs, etc.) and their sex partners or recipients of their "tainted" bodily fluids, to a disease transmitted by "risky activities" and not limited to groups or by national boundaries, to, finally, what the nature of the biological phenomenon AIDS is. Therefore, the first politicization was challenging the identification of homosexuality as the cause of AIDS.[16] Second, the movement problematized the societal institutionalization of the disease itself, based

---

"The Deadly Costs of an Obsession," *The Nation*, February 13, 1989, 181, 196–200, and the letters to the editor in response, "Gay Politics and AIDS," *The Nation*, March 20, 1989, 362, 277–79. See also Eric Rofes, "Gay Lib vs. AIDS: Averting Civil War in the 1990s," *Out/look* 8 (Spring 1990): 8–16.

15. At the risk of drawing a unilateral portrait of "the movement" (gay- and AIDS-activist) as a collective subject, here I refer to it as that combination of "membership organizations practicing lobbying and pressure group activities [and] participatory groups engaging in direct action" and individuals with self-developed expertise and rhetorical skills (such as Larry Kramer) who worked, sometimes cooperatively and sometimes conflictually, to use the window of opportunity of ignorance and public apathy about AIDS to empower themselves and to shape public policy during the epidemic. For a discussion of this point see Robert A. Padgug and Gerald M. Oppenheimer, "Riding the Tiger: AIDS and the Gay Community," in *AIDS: The Making of a Chronic Disease*, ed. Elizabeth Fee and Daniel Fox (Berkeley and Los Angeles: University of California Press), 245–78, at 272.

16. The political problem of defining the nature of the disease by giving it a name reflects this process. In little more than five years, the term for the disease evolved from GRID (gay related immune deficiency), to ACIDS (acquired community immune deficiency syndrome), to CAIDS (community acquired immune deficiency syndrome), to AIDS

upon what was considered knowledge about AIDS and who possessed that knowledge (AIDS expertise). Thus, the movement politicized "*managing* the crisis, turning the crisis into a condition, something that is part of the way things are . . . like a flood or hurricanes, or poverty"[17] rather than *stopping* it, what I referred to earlier as the cancerization of AIDS as a chronic disease. Third, and last, the movement problematized, in "everyday life," the specific instances of exercising power that the epidemic enabled. I will now analyze each of these three elements of the politicization of AIDS.

In the first instance, politicization transforms what was perceived as solely a medical problem into a political one, *a politicization of the activity of biomedical and epidemiological research.* This happened through a rejection of the "lifestyle hypothesis" of immune system compromise in favor of an "infectious agent hypothesis" of causation and the consequent reconceptualization of AIDS as a general, even global, public health problem, and through the expansion of the epidemiological profile of the disease syndrome from one that affected only gay men, to one also affecting intravenous (IV) drug users, to one that potentially affects everyone who has sex or is exposed subcutaneously to certain bodily fluids of another human be-

(acquired immune deficiency syndrome). An international agreement on nomenclature for the virus believed to cause it (from HTLV-III, to LAV, to "HIV infection" followed mutual U.S. and French accusations of scientific fraud. This is reported in Randy Shilts, *And the Band Played On: People, Politics, and the AIDS Epidemic* (New York: St. Martin's Press, 1989), 138, 171, and 593.

17. Larry Kramer, *Reports from the Holocaust: The Making of an AIDS Activist* (New York: St. Martin's Press, 1989), 258 (emphasis in original).

ing.[18] In order to accomplish this transformation in the order of "truth" of what AIDS was—how it constitutes a *disease,* what caused it, who had it—gay and lesbian physicians and scientific researchers, as well as community leaders, criticized what was *then* believed to cause the disease and the methodology for discovering its prevalence in the population as being based upon etiology and epidemiology that was compromised by scientists' prejudice against gay men. This rendered the lifestyle hypothesis suspect—as inadequate to a scientific conceptualization of disease. The redefinition of the disease through a different etiology and symptomatology contributed to a transformation in the ratio of gay to nongay cases reported in the urban United States, to the discovery of pandemic of heterosexually transmitted AIDS in Africa and other parts of the world, and to a retrospective diagnosis of cases, dubbed "junkie pneumonia" during the 1970s, that antedated the first ones found among gay men.

This politicization of the "scientific truth" about AIDS occurs at two other loci. First, the HIV hypothesis was questioned by movement journalists and physicians and even by some nongay scientists. They asked whether HIV is the sole cause of AIDS, or even a cause at all, focusing upon the role of economic motivations, institutional power (state regulative and funding processes, influential scientific-academic net-

18. For an analysis of the transformation within the medical profession from the "lifestyle hypothesis" into the "infectious-agent hypothesis," see Gerald M. Oppenheimer, "In the Eye of the Storm: The Epidemiological Construction of AIDS," in *AIDS: The Burdens of History*, ed. Elizabeth Fee and Daniel M. Fox (Berkeley and Los Angeles: University of California Press, 1988), 267–300.

works, etc.), and cultural hegemony in the production of scientific knowledge.[19] Second, the research-and-development priorities of state and academic laboratories and pharmaceutical enterprises were politicized in order to find a cure and treatments for the disease, not just a vaccine. This is *political* in that AIDS activists have had to organize well enough to be able to give assurances of financial gain to pharmaceutical corporations and to be able to pressure public institutions to do the basic scientific and epidemiological work on AIDS, on the view that it was a genuine *public* health problem, even when many argued that, since it appeared to be limited to "risk groups" and

19. Principal challengers of the HIV hypothesis of single-agent causation include Charles Ortleb, publisher of *New York Native*, a gay weekly, and Peter Duesberg, a microbiologist at the University of California at Berkeley. Summaries of their views, respectively, may be found in Katie Leishman, "The Outsider," *Rolling Stone*, March 23, 1989, 75; and John Lauritsen, "Saying No to HIV: An Interview with Professor Peter Duesberg," *Christopher Street*, no. 118 (December 1987): 17–34. A detailed criticism of the acceptance of the HIV hypothesis as an example of hegemony in the production of scientific knowledge may be found in Jad Adams, *AIDS: The HIV Myth* (New York: St. Martin's Press, 1989). As of 1993, some individuals are suggesting a redefinition similar to the lifestyle-to-virus one, from AIDS as caused solely by HIV to a broader definition of AIDS that would include CFIDS (chronic fatigue immune deficiency syndrome) as caused perhaps by a different virus, HHV-6. See Neenyah Ostrom, "Even Gallo May Soon Have to Admit that HHV-6 Is the Cause of 'AIDS' and Chronic Fatigue Syndrome," *New York Native*, no. 521:1, 6. The underlying presupposition of this hypothesis is that when AIDS is diagnosed in U.S. minority populations (e.g., gay men, African Americans, intravenous drug users, Haitian immigrants) it is called AIDS as caused by HIV infection; when it is diagnosed in the white middle-class population, it is called CFIDS ("yuppie flu") of an unknown etiology. According to this hypothesis, these are really manifestations on a continuum of the same disease—"AIDS major" and "AIDS minor"—caused by HHV-6, which then allows for infection by HIV and progression of HIV disease as an opportunistic infection. There is also challenge to the HIV hypothesis by groups organized internationally; the most active is Group for the Scientific Reappraisal of the HIV-AIDS Hypothesis, which includes scientists and Nobel laureates.

"known modes of transmission," the so-called general public was devoting a disproportionate amount of scarce socioeconomic resources to it.[20] Thus, and simultaneously, the *definition* of AIDS has progressively been challenged to account for who was actually becoming ill: hemophiliacs and other recipients of blood products; intravenous drug users, their sexual partners, and their offspring; heterosexuals, first in Africa, then in other (particularly poorer) parts of the world; even those suffering from CFIDS (chronic fatigue immune deficiency syndrome). As the kinds of infections that define AIDS have increased (along with the aggregate number of cases), so has its definition through epidemiology and etiology been challenged.

As distinct from AIDS science, the second object of politicization is the *institutionalization of AIDS* through the development of biotechnologies and through consequent norms of health that are enforced by both public and private methods. Undergirding this is the institutionalization of the HIV hypothesis. Scientists and public-health officials have predicted that the epidemic will continue for twenty to thirty years and that those currently infected with the putative cause, HIV, or those who become infected will incubate the virus and be infectious for the rest of their lives. This enables testing members of so-called high-risk groups for the determination of health status, as

20. The last perspective appears to inform the argument of Tomas J. Philipson and Richard A. Posner, *Private Choices and Public Health* (Cambridge, Mass.: Harvard University Press, 1993). The "containment" view of the epidemic in the United States is in National Research Council, *The Social Impact of AIDS in the United States* (Washington: National Academy Press, 1993). This view has been criticized by those who question how the definition of AIDS has been constructed.

well as permanent medical monitoring to prevent the progression of the viral infection and permanent monitoring of lifestyle to promote "good behavior," as AIDS researcher Robert Gallo put it in 1989.[21] Testing, treatment, and monitoring would take place under the guidance of physicians and other experts who have the latest diagnostic, treatment, and risk-management knowledge and the process would involve an archipelago of institutions for medical surveillance and intervention, as well as for individual behavior modification. Further, AIDS activists, arguing from "compassionate use," have pressed government regulatory agencies for speedy approval of new biotechnologies. But many people living with the prospect of imminent death because of the definition of AIDS as a terminal illness intervene early based upon exposure to HIV and an abnormally low level of "T-cells"—a part of the immune system. They take a progression and variety of drugs of unknown toxicities in the hope of extending their lives. Thus, the definition of AIDS as a terminal disease, and the biotechnologies developed to stave off "the inevitable," institutionalize AIDS—they have moved it away from the epidemic paradigm to the chronic-disease paradigm. In addition to this institutionalization of AIDS because of its etiology (HIV), symptomatology (list of opportunistic infections), and epidemiology (populations "at risk" of infection with HIV), AIDS expertise—who can speak the truth about AIDS—was also politicized. Thus, the independence—intellectual and economical—of medi-

---

21. Anthony Liversidge, "AIDS: Words from the Front," *Spin* 4(12) (March 1989): 61.

cal doctors has been problematized and different kinds of expertise have been constructed. These include self-taught PWAs and AIDS activists, those people steeped in knowledge of "alternative health" models (alternative to those of medical biotechnologies), and people who subscribe to competing theories of AIDS etiology.

Third, the result of the institutionalization of AIDS and the construction of expertise about it is a further *anatomo-political (over individual bodies) and biopolitical (over populations) exercise of power* through sexuality. However, its coding is personal-and public-health imperatives that are thereby able to contradict and sometimes circumvent legal limitations on the exercise of state power to accomplish their health goals. Such power is authorized by law; although the forms through which it is exercised are sometimes judicial, they more often involve administrative rulings and public-health regulations that are adaptable to changing scientific knowledge about what constitutes a medical risk. The goal of government, both as official policies and as the ordering of one's own life according to norms promulgated by health experts, is to enable individuals and the populations within which they have been constructed (e.g., sexually active gay men within the "gay male community," "men who have sex with men" but do not identify themselves as belonging to that community, intravenous drug users and the population of individuals who are their sexual partners, etc.) to realize their potential as living beings. This is achieved through a biological objectification of humans and their environment (as "AIDS"—as an "epidemic" or as a "chronic disease" condition—itself is such an objectification). From this perspective, every individual is a kind of biological risk factor for others, and government becomes a question not so much of protecting each individual from attack by others (as in classical liberal theory) but of risk management. On the one side, programs of government, whether those using state coercion or those that are voluntary and "community-based," must manage populations so as to preserve them against biological threats from within. On the other side, such programs must make sure that the population realizes its potential—that each individual behaves in as prophylactic a manner as possible and, to ensure that this is so, that each individual account for and assume responsibility for the management of her or his own life or "lifestyle."

Following from the foregoing, specific power relations in "everyday life" that have been enabled by AIDS have been politicized. A "politics of AIDS" problematizes the exercise of power by people *who would tell us how to live* through their knowledge, mentioned above, of risk factors for contracting the disease, through their medical knowledge of how to preserve the lives of those who have the disease, and through their knowledge of how to "cope" with the cultural manifestations of the disease. All of these "pastoral" forms of power operate primarily through techniques of subjection. Within a situation of domination by the scientific "truth about AIDS," the institutionalization of this truth as biomedical technique and expertise, and "commonsense" psychological or moral principles, they try to get individuals to follow certain rules of sexual and medical conduct that, they are told, will assure their salvation.[22] In this context, the individuals included are the sick, those who have tested HIV-positive, and the "worried well"; the politicized relationships include those of physician or psychotherapist and patient (where medical dependency and psychosexual tutelage is at stake) and that of social worker and client (where the removal of the client from coverage by the state is at stake). Thus, while not mandatory in a formal sense, these procedures of subjection are buttressed by a domination of the form: what is at stake—according to expert knowledge—is the continuation of your own life.

While being hold how one should live one's life by psycho-medical experts is characteristic of modern biopower, what is specific to the politics of AIDS is the content of such statements, to the extent it is generated by expertise from the lesbian and gay community and allows for continuous give and take between the "expert" and the ones about whom the "expertise" is garnered. Indeed, it was through a politicization of the expert-client relationship and the development of gay and lesbian community-based expertise (particularly about clinical treatment research and legal questions

22. See, for example, theoretical work such as Cindy Patton, *Inventing AIDS* (New York and London: Routledge, 1990), and practical manuals such as Martin Delaney and Peter Goldblum, with Joseph Brewer, *Strategies for Survival: A Gay Men's Health Manual for the Age of AIDS* (New York: St. Martin's Press, 1987); and John S. James, *AIDS Treatment News: Issues 1 through 75* and *Issues 76 through 125* (Berkeley: Celestial Arts, 1989, 1991) and *Issues 126 through 189* (Boston: Alyson Publications, 1994). For a theoretical discussion of "pastoral power," see Michel Foucault, "The Subject and Power," trans. Leslie Sawyer, an afterword in Hubert Dreyfus and Paul Rabinow, *Michel Foucault: Beyond Structuralism and Hermeneutics* (Chicago: University of Chicago Press, 1982), 214–15.

regarding AIDS care) that medical and other experts were able to be dealt with "on a basis of relative equality and prevent[ed] from simply imposing their interests, aims, and methodologies on the community and on individuals with AIDS."[23] This politicization transforms the power relationship by organizing patients and those who believe themselves "at risk" to produce, gather, and share information about the disease, by employing physicians from the gay community (who are often ill themselves) in self-monitored treatment and research experiments, and by developing safer sexual practices and educating others about them. The relation of social-service professionals (who want to monitor their clients' way of life) to individuals who claim benefits from the state has also been problematized.[24] This last element of the politicization of AIDS, that of the power exercised by health counselors and social-welfare personnel, has already resulted in a reorientation of health-care and social-service delivery systems during the epidemic. It suggests how medical techniques of government can be adapted and transformed by those over whom such power is being exercised (first gay men and, later, others affected by AIDS) to "demystify" existing knowledge and debate the production and content of new knowledge as well as force institutional flexibility so that such government through medicine can be more advi-

23. Padgug and Oppenheimer, "Riding the Tiger," 265.

24. For a discussion of the political significance of patient self-empowerment in the context of the AIDS epidemic, see Daniel Defert, "A New Social Reformer: The Patient," in *Behavioral Aspects of AIDS*, ed. David G. Ostrow (New York: Plenum, 1990), 1–6.

sory than authoritarian in relation to one's regimen of living.[25]

Indeed, as a direct result of the epidemic the lesbian and gay movement embarked on a process of institution building unsurpassed in its speed, I would conjecture, by any other social movement in modern history.[26] These institutions included groups created

---

25. In the United States, Gay Men's Health Crisis pioneered this movement of institution building, beginning in 1982, by providing public education about the nature of the epidemic, by developing educational programs on how to have safer sex, and by providing services for people with AIDS. Later, the People with AIDS Coalition was formed (and governed by and exclusively devoted to people who had AIDS); Body Positive followed for people who had tested positive for HIV infection. Project Inform on the West Coast and the AIDS Treatment Registry on the East Coast were founded by AIDS activists to disseminate information on treatments and research/treatment protocols. The Community Research Initiative on AIDS (CRIA) was set up—originally in violation of U.S. Food and Drug Administration regulations, and subsequently with that agency's blessing—to administer experimental drugs to seriously ill PWAs (people living with AIDS) under the close supervision of physicians based in the gay community. Treatment Action Group (TAG), originally part of ACT UP (AIDS Coalition to Unleash Power, a network of activist groups throughout the United States and abroad), became an activist organization to monitor corporate and state research and development on treatment. This list of prominent organizations in the two urban areas of the United States is far from exhaustive (key organizations also include the Terrence Higgins Trust in the U.K. and A.I.D.E.S. in France, founded by Defert). Finally, ACT UP has had rapid success in grass-roots organizing and demonstrating, in political education of its members and education of the public, and in influencing policy making regarding the epidemic. See AIDS Coalition to Unleash Power/New York, *The ACT UP Women's Caucus Women and AIDS Handbook* (New York, 1989); and AIDS Coalition to Unleash Power/New York, *A National AIDS Treatment Research Agenda*, a report prepared for the Fifth International Conference on AIDS, Montreal, June 1989 (New York, 1989) and for subsequent International Conferences on AIDS for exemplary position and strategy statements. Histories of AIDS organizations include Arthur D. Kahn, *AIDS: The Winter War* (Philadelphia: Temple University Press, 1993); Philip M. Kayal, *Bearing Witness: Gay Men's Health Crisis and the Politics of AIDS* (Boulder, Colo.: Westview Press, 1993); and, on French activism, Emmanuel Hirsch, *A.I.D.E.S. Solidaires* (Paris: Editions du Cerf, 1991).

26. The *institutional* history of the lesbian and gay movement from Stonewall (1969) to the present, and its comparison with twenty-five-

in direct response to the epidemic (concerned with patient services, lobbying, preventive health work, and public education) and institutions created or strengthened in response to the epidemic but less directly related to the disease itself (concerned with legal services, antigay defamation and violence, and creating local and national political action committees). In a sense, the epidemic forced the community back on itself, owing to the lack of democratic support, attributable to homophobia, for measures to stop the course of the disease. Again, and perhaps most important, politicization of AIDS has shown how people over whom biopower is exercised can, on an interpersonal level, build networks for individual support and collective action. This process results in the creation of new institutions, and the direction of existing ones, that problematize domains of life for medical knowledge on behalf of the needs for sexual health. Such institutions can then be used by individuals to take care of *themselves*, undermining domination. This is done by making the relationship between experts and those over whom power is exercised (based upon the expertise) open to questioning. The individuals who are the objects of power (and of the knowledge garnered to create the expertise), through anatamo-politics, can then be supported by the population groupings they comprise, by virtue of biopolitics, to challenge the truth claims of the experts and affect the power exercised over them.

---

year periods for other movements, has yet to be written; but locally, nationally, and internationally the sheer number of institutions created during this period is staggering.

The politics of AIDS has shown how the institutions of the gay and lesbian community, by taking "ownership" of AIDS as their issue in the context of homophobic policy assertion (as well as distancing from and lack of mobilization around the issue by other affected communities), have empowered the lesbian and gay community through grassroots mobilization, institution building, and advisory participation in public and corporate decision making. What historical analysis will determine is how successful such a politics of the life sciences can be (the U.S. Manhattan Project to create the atom bomb is held up as a positive example by U.S. AIDS activists for finding the cure for AIDS). It should be successful, some argue, since what a disease is *understood* to be is socially constructed and therefore it should be eliminable through the application of political will. Yet by 1994, after thirteen years, although PWAs are living longer, little gain has been made in saving their lives, and people continue to be diagnosed with AIDS. Until this situation changes, the ethico-erotic imperatives of gay men and lesbians, as historically indicated, will ensure that AIDS remains a political issue.

As an assertion of "lesbian and gay rights," the politics of AIDS is framed as a third "moment" of contemporary lesbian and gay politics: that of equity. Constitution of oneself through one's erotic relations—that is, ethics, the making of oneself into an agent of one's actions—means a claim upon the resources of society in order to do so. (Others who invent themselves through religious means benefit by the society's protection of their freedom to do so, not the least by not having their institutionalized expression taxed by the state.) Thus, gay and lesbian rights includes a right to have access to the means of sexual hygiene in one's relationships with others—a relational right. Gays and lesbians contribute to society in ways that disproportionately benefit others: for example, gays and lesbians without children pay taxes to educate the children of those, nongays *and* gays, who procreate. While another way of framing this issue would be on the administrative model of social insurance—all pay for benefits that they may or may not come to need—the stronger argument is the one from equity, based upon a right to have the affective relationships one chooses in order to create one's selfhood.[27]

Conclusion

I end this chapter with the "Platform of the 1993 March on Washington for Lesbian, Gay, and Bi[sexual] Equal Rights and Liberation." The march was a "demonstration" to, and the demands were directed at, society as a whole rather than simply to the agencies of the state headquartered in the U.S. capital.

---

27. Thus, in the dissent to *Bowers v. Hardwick* (1986), where the U.S. Supreme Court upheld Georgia's statute forbidding homosexual sex as sodomy: "Sexual intimacy is a sensitive, key relationship of human existence, central to family life, community welfare, and the development of human personality. . . . The fact that individuals define themselves in a significant way through their intimate sexual relationships with others suggests, in a Nation as diverse as ours, that there may be many 'right' ways of conducting those relationships, and that much of the richness of a relationship will come from the freedom an individual has to *choose* the form and nature of these intensely personal bonds. . . . It is precisely because the issue raised by this case touches the heart of what makes individuals what they are that we should be especially sensitive to the rights of those whose choices upset the majority" (emphasis in original).

Allow me to contextualize this event through the theoretical framework for lesbian and gay rights that I have already elaborated.

Lesbian and gay rights are asserted toward a technology of power in contemporary society that has emerged since the nineteenth century. It is a source of oppression, understood as domination by institutionalized heterosexism. Homophobic individuals are raised, and then rewarded, to maintain the dominant structure of heterosexist power by procedures of subjection that construct the truth about the self through self-examination and verbalization about one's sexuality that then open up pathways for power to be exercised over that self.

This oppression results from the installation of sexual relationships into a regime of truth such that heterosexual relationships are true, normal, and healthy, but homosexual ones are errors—abnormal, unhealthy, or sinful. These latter, to the extent that heterosexist power allows them to become socially visible, are often stigmatized and become the "living proof" of the truth of the heterosexual ones (what other theorists have called their "supplement").[28] More often, they are *disallowed*—the specific treatment of homosexuality has been to render it invisible by denying such relationships institutional status and, through the power of subjection, coercively shape individuals to "closet" themselves, thereby making them socially dead.

---

28. Eve Kosofsky Sedgwick, "Queer Performativity: Henry James's *The Art of the Novel*," *GLQ: A Journal of Lesbian and Gay Studies* 1(1): 1–16, at 3.

Lesbian and gay rights begins by challenging why sexual relations need be intelligible as a matter for truth claims about the congruence between social organization and a "deep" self at all, rather than being simply that to which partners mutually agree, within the bounds of safety, and limited by one's sovereignty over oneself. As such, erotic relationships are a way one invents oneself, in that work-in-progress that is one's life—they are primarily an aesthetic, not a verdical, matter (even though the ethical self-creation involves different *kinds* of truth claims than those of compulsory heterosexuality).

Then, lesbian and gay rights can be conceived as a relational right—our "right to love" which seems to incorporate the three "moments" of rights strategy. This involves the right to the use of one's body—erotically—in the constitution of oneself through relations with others.[29] It involves claims upon the normative order of society of equal validity for erotic self-constitution (which would include legal and social recognition of the varied relationships that coalesce through erotics) as for other means of ethical constitution. And it involves distributive justice because since erotic relationships are themselves intrinsically valuable to the individual and society-as-a-whole, one has a right to equity, a fair share of society's fostering in

29. "Privacy" then becomes, more aptly, the right to develop oneself through one's sexuality, as in what one strain of the nineteenth-century German gay movement called itself—Community of Self-Owners (alternatively translated as the Community of the Special). Many of their ethical arguments, however developed historically to counter biological determinism, are reflective of a conservative right-to-privacy strategy. See *Homosexuality and Male Bonding in Pre-Nazi Germany*, ed. Hubert Kennedy and Harry Oosterhuis (New York: Harrington Park Press, 1991), especially the discussion on 22–23, note 10.

engaging in them, at the very least, through access to the means of sexual health.

Turning finally to the demands of the March on Washington, they embody the assertion of lesbian and gay relational rights with regard to how the truth of sexuality has been constructed and institutionalized, and how it has programmed the exercise of power since the nineteenth century. This program occurred, recall: (1) through positing a sexual instinct and its perversion; (2) through the political socialization of procreation; (3) through the pedagogization of children's sexuality; and (4) through hysterization of women, and indeed, the constitution and iteration of gender inequality. The March on Washington document: (1) through the inclusion of bisexuals, challenges the teleological grounding of sexuality as an instinct; (2) defines "family" relationally on the basis of affinities chosen through erotics rather than through biological reproduction, decentering the heterosexual couple as the primary social unit; (3) expands the pedagogization of children's sexuality in a developmental, child-centered way, allowing for homoerotic and gender-nonconforming potentiality and the reality of children raised by lesbian and gay parents; and (4) by the inclusion of transgender and cross-gender as a component of the freedom of expression of sexual identity, eliminates dimorphic biological sex or gender as the ground of what sexuality is at all. What sexuality consists in, according to this document, is left to individuals inventing themselves within and through their erotic relationships with each other.

Figure 3. Platform of the 1993 March on Washington for Lesbian, Gay, and Bi Equal Rights and Liberation

Action Statement Preamble to the Platform

The Lesbian, Gay, Bisexual and Transgender movement recognizes that our quest for social justice fundamentally links us to the struggles against racism and sexism, class bias, economic injustice and religious intolerance. We must realize if one of us is oppressed we all are oppressed. The diversity of our movement requires and compels us to stand in opposition to all forms of oppression that diminish the quality of life for all people. We will be vigilant in our determination to rid our movement and our society of all forms of oppression and exploitation, so that all of us can develop to our full human potential without regard to race, religion, sexual orientation/identification, identity, gender and gender expression, ability, age or class.

The March Demands

1. We demand passage of a Lesbian, Gay, Bisexual, and Transgender civil rights bill and an end to discrimination by state and federal governments including the military; repeal of all sodomy laws and other laws that criminalize private sexual expression between consenting adults.

2. We demand massive increase in funding for AIDS education, research, and patient care; universal access to health care including alternative therapies; and an end to sexism in medical research and health care.

3. We demand legislation to prevent discrimination against Lesbians, Gays, Bisexuals and Transgendered people in the areas of family diversity, custody, adoption and foster care and that the definition of family includes the full diversity of all family structures.

4. We demand full and equal inclusion of Lesbians, Gays, Bisexuals and Transgendered people in the educational system, and inclusion of Lesbian, Gay, Bisexual and Transgender studies in multicultural curricula.

5. We demand the right to reproductive freedom and choice, to control our own bodies, and an end to sexist discrimination.

6. We demand an end to racial and ethnic discrimination in all forms.

7. We demand an end to discrimination and violent oppression based on actual or perceived sexual orientation/identification, race, reli-

gion, identity, sex and gender expression, disability, age, class, AIDS/HIV infection.

Platform Demands and Related Items

1. We demand passage of a Lesbian, Gay, Bisexual and Transgender civil rights bill and an end to discrimination by state and federal governments including the military; repeal of all sodomy laws and other laws that criminalize private sexual expression between consenting adults.

   Passage of "The Civil Rights Amendment Act of 1991" (HR 1430 & S574).

   Repeal of Department of Defense directive 1332.14.

   Repeal of laws prohibiting sodomy, cross-gender expression (dress codes) or non-coercive sexual behavior between consenting adults.

   Amendment of the Code of Federal Regulations to recognize same-sex relationships.

   Passage of the Equal Rights Amendment

   Implementation of, funding for and enforcement of the Americans with Disabilities Act of 1991.

   Passage and implementation of graduated age-of-consent laws.

2. We demand massive increase in funding for AIDS education, research, and patient care; universal access to health care including alternative therapies; and an end to sexism in medical research and health care.

   The provision of responsive, appropriate health care for people with disabilities, deaf and hard of hearing people.

   Revision of the Centers for Disease Control definition of AIDS to include infections particular to women.

   Implementation of the recommendation of the National AIDS Commission immediately.

   A massive increase in funding for AIDS education, research and care—money for AIDS, not for war. This money should come from the defense budget, not existing social services.

   An increase in funding and research to provide an independent study of HIV infection in women, People of Color, Bisexuals, Heterosexuals, children, and women to women transmission.

   Access to anonymous testing for HIV.

   No mandatory HIV testing.

   A cure for AIDS.

   The development and legalization of a national needle exchange program.

   Free substance abuse treatment on demand.

The re-definition of sexual re-assignment surgeries as medical, not cosmetic, treatment.

The provision of appropriate medical treatment for all transgendered people in prisons and hospitals.

An increase in funding and research for chronic illness, including breast, ovarian, and other cancers particular to women.

The right of all people with chronic illness, including HIV/AIDS, to choices in medical treatment as well as the right to end such treatment.

3. We demand legislation to prevent discrimination against Lesbians, Gays, Bisexuals and Transgendered people in the areas of family diversity, custody, adoption and foster care and that the definition of family includes the full diversity of all family structures.

   The recognition and legal protection of whole range of family structures.

   An end to abuse and exploitation of and discrimination against youth.

   An end to abuse and exploitation of and discrimination against older/old people.

   Full implementation of the recommendations contained in the report of the Health and Human Services Task Force on Youth Suicide.

   Recognition of domestic partnerships.

   Legalization of same sex marriages.

4. We demand full and equal inclusion of Lesbians, Gays, Bisexuals and Transgendered people in the educational system, and inclusion of Lesbian, Gay, Bisexual and Transgender studies in multicultural curricula.

   Culturally inclusive Lesbian, Gay, Bisexual and Transgender Studies program; and information on abortion, AIDS/HIV, childcare and sexuality at all levels of education.

   Establishment of campus offices and programs to address Lesbian, Gay, Bisexual and Transgender students' special needs.

   The ban of all discriminatory ROTC programs and recruiters from learning institutions.

   An end to discrimination at all levels of education.

5. We demand the right to reproductive freedom and choice, to control our own bodies, and an end to sexist discrimination.

   The right to control our bodies.

   Unrestricted, safe and affordable alternative insemination.

   An end to sterilization abuse.

   That access to safe and affordable abortion and contraception be available to all people on demand, without restriction and regardless of age.

That access to unbiased and complete information about the full range of reproductive options be available to all people, regardless of age.

6. We demand an end to racial and ethnic discrimination in all forms.

   Support for non-racist policies and affirmative action.

   An end to institutionalized racism.

   Equal economic opportunity and an end to poverty.

   Full reproductive rights, improvement of pre-natal services, availability of alternative insemination for Lesbians and Bisexual women of color.

   Repeal all 'English Only' laws and restore and enforce bilingual education.

   Repeal all discriminatory immigration laws based on race and HIV status.

   A commitment to ending racism, including internalized racism, sexism and all forms of religious and ethnic oppression in our communities and in this country.

   An end to the genocide of all the indigenous peoples and their cultures.

   Restoration of the self-determination of all indigenous people of the world.

7. We demand an end to discrimination and violent oppression based on actual or perceived sexual orientation/identification, race, religion, identity, sex and gender expression, disability, age, class, AIDS/HIV infection.

   An end to anti-Semitism.

   An end to sexist oppression.

   An end to discrimination against people with disabilities, deaf and hard of hearing people.

   An end to discrimination based on sexual orientation in all programs of the Boy Scouts of America.

   An end to economic injustice in this country and internationally.

   An end to discrimination against prisoners with HIV/AIDS.

   An end to discrimination against people with HIV/AIDS, and those perceived as having HIV/AIDS.

   An end to consideration of gender dysphoria as a psychiatric disorder.

   An end to hate crimes including police brutality, rape and bashing.

   An end to censorship.

Chapter 5

An Ethos of Lesbian and Gay Existence

I am out, therefore I am.

From a sticker (designed by Adam Rolston) posted around New York City during Gay and Lesbian Pride Month, June 1989

Politics, finally, involves problematizing, calling into question, power relations in society *by* a social movement, *through* transformation of techniques that are used to govern people—exercising and submitting to power relations—and a production of knowledge (writing, reflection, scientific or other statements that make claims to truth) about the meaning of this phenomenon *as* political. In this chapter I analyze primarily the last aspect of this activity of politicization, the production of knowledge by the contemporary lesbian and gay movement. However, the analysis will deal by implication with the other components of politicization, for the political knowledge that the movement is producing is both constitutive of and an expression of what I call an ethos of lesbian and gay existence. Thus, the knowledge produced through this ethos at once gives meaning to lesbian and gay existence as political and is a form and site of resistance within hegemonic relationships of power in contemporary society; as such, it influences them.

I begin by arguing that lesbian and gay existence should be conceived as an ethos rather than as a sexual preference or orientation, as a lifestyle, or *primarily* in collectivist terms, as a subculture, or even as a community. While lesbian and gay existence may include some elements of these conceptualizations, "ethos" is a more encompassing formulation, better suited for comprehending lesbian and gay existence politically. I argue that the key to understanding ethos lies in the lesbian and gay conceptualization of "coming out," understood as a process of *becoming* in which the individual enters into the field of relationships that constitute the lesbian and gay community. Through this process, she or he participates in a collective problematization of self, of types of normativity, and of what counts as truth. It is in the relationship that the individual creates with her- or himself and with others in this practice of the self that is called "coming out" that an ethos emerges. Finally, this lesbian and gay ethos, or way of life, is a source for a new ethic that has implications for politics generally.

I use as my point of departure here the words of Eve Kosofsky Sedgwick: "The *special* centrality of homophobic oppression in the twentieth century . . . has resulted from its inextricability from the question of knowledge and the processes of knowing in modern

Western culture at large."[1] Nevertheless, as I have discussed, knowledge is a qualification through which power can and must be exercised in contemporary society. Therefore, the knowledge that is a product of lesbian and gay political problematization may well be a way of protecting oneself from homophobia taken to its genocidal extreme, as in the complete elimination of homosexuality or of homosexuals. I use the adjective "genocidal" advisedly, and not hyperbolically (even the former Surgeon General of the United States, C. Everett Koop, spoke of the possibility of homosexual genocide in the context of the AIDS epidemic).[2] One conceptualization of genocide (with which Doctor Koop might agree), drawn from the experience of the epidemic, is that of the U.S. social historian Robert Dawidoff: "Genocide does not ever happen in the same way to the same people, but it always means the wiping out of a despised people through active malevolence or the manipulation of the accidental, plus the denial of its targeted community, and the indifference of the world and its acquiescence in the horror."[3]

However, even this conceptualization is misleading—it requires subjective intentionality from those

1. Eve Kosofsky Sedgwick, *Epistemology of the Closet* (Berkeley and Los Angeles: University of California Press, 1990), 33–34 (emphasis in original).

2. The former surgeon general's use of the concept is in Maureen Dowd, "Dr. Koop Defends His Crusade on AIDS," *New York Times*, April 16, 1987, B8.

3. Robert Dawidoff, "Memorial Day, 1988," in *Personal Dispatches: Writers Confront AIDS*, ed. John Preston (New York: St. Martin's Press, 1989), 177. For a historical analysis of the Nazi extermination of gays, see Richard Plant, *The Pink Triangle: The Nazi War against Homosexuals* (New York: Henry Holt, 1986).

who "target" a particular community. The systemic obliteration of populations is an ever-present possibility of modern government where power is exercised as biopower, that is, across two axes of human existence—anatomically through individual bodies, and biologically through the populations that they comprise—and where the processes of life become the object of modern techniques of government, which exercise power to foster life or to disallow it to the point of death. In the context of this historical development, knowledge is produced by lesbians and gay men both to be set against culturally endemic homophobic distortion and to reveal and stop the institutionalized disallowance of their lives (as well as to demonstrate how those lives can be fostered).

It is this historical imperative to produce the truth of and for one's own existence that motivates me; however, this is not to say that truth in and of itself can protect me or anyone else. The limitations of the knowledge produced by the lesbian and gay movement are obvious to any lesbian or gay person. For example, when the psychiatric definition of homosexuality as illness was overturned through political problematization of the power of psychiatrists by the lesbian and gay movement, the AIDS epidemic then allowed for the remedicalization of homosexual sex as disease producing, generating yet another political problematization through AIDS activism. If truth is created through communal life as an objectification of shared values, then the creation of truth—not only about lesbian and gay existence but, from the vantage point of that existence, about what politics *is* today—refocuses contemporary human reality in a new way.

What will protect lesbians and gay men and enable them to flourish is an ethos that serves as a condition of possibility for politics, understood both as the creation of community among and between lesbians and gay men and as the transformation of institutionalized power relations to the extent that lesbians and gay men visibly occupy positions of sociocultural power and authority. Thus, what is significant in the production of knowledge by the lesbian and gay movement is not only an antihomophobic discourse (Sedgwick's project) but also the way in which a lesbian and gay ethos produces knowledge that transforms the political world and the way all people understand themselves as living in that world.

Lesbian and Gay Existence: Sexual Orientation, Lifestyle, and Community

My claim is that living as a lesbian or a gay man today consists in more than a sexual orientation, a lifestyle, or even being a member of a community. It consists in an ethos—a shared way of life through which lesbians and gay men invent themselves, recognize each other, and establish a relationship to the culture in which they live. Before analyzing the emergence of a distinctive lesbian and gay ethos, I discuss the limitations of the conventional ways of understanding lesbian and gay existence today.

Sexual Preference or Alternative Lifestyle?

"Sexual preference," for example, suggests that same-sex erotics is merely analogous to one's preference for a particular flavor of ice cream, and that lesbians and gay men are the same as nongays except for what they do in bed. If this were true, there would be no need for the institutions of the lesbian and gay community. These have been built specifically to counter oppression and to create safe spaces wherein women can come out as lesbians and meet each other and men can come out as gay and meet each other too, by means of activities that extend far beyond sexual encounters. If the term "sexual preference" is trivializing, then "sexual orientation," rooted as it is in the psychiatric discourse that formerly posited homosexuality as a mental illness, suggests that sexual object choice is fixed at a very early age, perhaps prenatally or through genetic predisposition, and is therefore not amenable to change except through extraordinary means. The orientation hypothesis may or may not be etiologically true. Since many people who are "oriented" toward their own sex may not act out this orientation or may do so only furtively, what is important (as in nature/nurture discourse generally) is what one *does* with this orientation, how one "works on" one's sexuality, as I demonstrated in the discussion of lesbian and gay erotics in Chapter 3. This is why I have chosen Adrienne Rich's formulation of lesbian and gay *existence*: it indicates the historical fact of the presence of people who understand themselves as lesbian and gay, as well as their continuing creation of the meaning of that existence.[4]

---

4. David Halperin historically traces the conceptual referent of "orientation," if not the word itself, to Carl Friedrich Otto Westphal's "diagnosis" of "contrary sexual feeling" that "does not always coincidentally concern the sexual drive as such but simply the feeling of being alienated, with one's entire inner being, from one's own sex—a less

Further, it is not just homosexual sexual acts themselves that precipitate the fear and hatred of those who engage in this kind of sexual behavior on the part of those who do not; rather, it is what these latter people call the "gay lifestyle." Such a fear and hatred may be manifest on the level of individual "homosexual panic" (the fear that one will lose one's gender identity)[5] or in the anxiety that the gay lifestyle, ultimately a stereotype, is causing the downfall of Western civilization. An example of the latter are the comments of Norman Podhoretz on the "central role homosexuality played" in the interwar period in England. Upper-class youths, in schools where only "state-subsidized undergraduates [were] generally heterosexual," "dandies," and

> aesthetes . . . through their writings, their political activities, and the way of life they followed . . . added to the antidemocratic pacifism of the interwar ethos: a generalized contempt for middle-class or indeed any kind of heterosexual adult life.

developed stage, as it were, of the pathological phenomenon." Westphal is cited in David Halperin, *One Hundred Years of Homosexuality and Other Essays on Greek Love* (New York: Routledge, 1990), 163, note 52. My conceptualization of lesbian and gay existence is informed by Adrienne Rich, "Compulsory Heterosexuality and Lesbian Existence," in *Powers of Desire: The Politics of Sexuality*, ed. Ann Snitow, Christine Stansell, and Sharon Thompson (New York: Monthly Review Press, 1983), 192.

5. The relationship between gender and sexuality, as it motivates homosexual panic, is too complex to discuss here. Also, the literature on male homosexual panic is more developed than that on its female counterpart. An interesting structural approach to the former is Eve Kosofsky Sedgwick, *Between Men: English Literature and Male Homosocial Desire* (New York: Columbia University Press, 1986), 83–96, and *Epistemology*, 182–212.

> For whatever else homosexuality may be or may be caused by, to these young men of the English upper class it represented . . . the refusal of fatherhood and all that fatherhood entailed: responsibility for a family and therefore an inescapable implication in the destiny of society as a whole. And that so many of the privileged young of England "no longer wanted to grow up to become fathers themselves" also meant that they were repudiating their birthright as successors to their own fathers in assuming a direct responsibility for the fate of the country.
>
> Anyone familiar with homosexual apologetics in America today will recognize these attitudes.[6]

A resentful Midge Decter, writing in the same publication, reveals (indeed, endorses) the stereotyping of a gay lifestyle. Decrying the "mocking effect on heterosexuals . . . of homosexual style, invented by homosexuals and serving the purpose of domination by ridicule," she implores her readers to "*know them as a group*. . . . One cannot even begin to get at *the truth about homosexuals* without this kind of generalization."[7]

No other aspect of the existence of lesbians and gay men comes under such intense scrutiny by others as that of their lifestyle. Even if the criticism is not as homophobic as that cited above, it often seems to imply that lesbians and gay men constitute some exotic non-Western tribe newly discovered by anthropologists and sensationalized by the media. Their "life-

6. Norman Podhoretz, "The Culture of Appeasement," *Commentary* 64(4) (October 1977): 30, 31.

7. Midge Decter, "The Boys on the Beach," *Commentary* 70(3) (September 1980): 39, 40–41 (emphasis mine).

style" is simultaneously the point upon which gay and lesbian people are attacked most frequently by non-gays and central to the movement's problematic of what it means to be lesbian or gay. It is through this problematization of their putative "lifestyle" that the possibility of an ethos emerges, having as much importance as freedom of erotic choices and the struggle for lesbian and gay legal rights. What is at stake is not simply a sexual orientation or an alternative lifestyle (one among others in the context of a pluralistic culture), but the question "How shall I live?"

There are other significant reasons for the intense questioning by lesbians and gay men themselves of their own manner of existing. The condition of compulsory heterosexuality, what Christopher Isherwood called "the heterosexual dictatorship," makes simply living every day a serious problem for lesbians and gay men. Laws, forms of culture (rituals, symbols, etc.), and the most mundane social expectations make one an alien in the world. It is for this reason that the "gay ghetto" exists. Gay and lesbian commercial establishments, social institutions, neighborhoods, resorts, and cruising areas constitute a "liberated zone" where lesbians and gay men can feel at home in and at peace with the world. Much the same is true of cultural "spaces" or events involving art, music festivals, lesbian and gay literature, athletic leagues, conferences, and informational and friendship networks like those arising through AIDS activism. To be sure, the ghetto exists because lesbians and gay men, to the extent that they come out, have been forced by societal rejection to find other means of livelihood, other sources of emotional sustenance, and other institutional frameworks within which to pursue their life objectives. The gay ghetto is significantly a manifestation of forced ghettoization.

Nevertheless, the birth, since the Stonewall Riots of 1969, of a lesbian and gay counterculture within the stifling larger culture is something of an illusion. Most lesbians and gay men do not live in a gay ghetto,[8] and the possibility of establishing a gay nation-state is unlikely and probably unwise. Some gay analysis even sees nationalism as part and parcel of the logic of social reproduction and a growth economy dependent upon heterosexuality, biological reproduction, and generational transmission of culture and capital, in which the self would be fulfilled *through* identification with these processes.[9] Gay men and lesbians are

---

8. For accounts of the diversity of ways of living as a lesbian or a gay man throughout the United States, see Neil Miller, *In Search of Gay America* (New York: Atlantic Monthly Press, 1989); Martha Barron Barrett, *Invisible Lives: The Truth about Millions of Women Loving Women* (New York: William Morrow, 1989); and (for an earlier account) Edmund White, *States of Desire: Travels in Gay America* (New York: E. P. Dutton, 1980).

9. This is the hypothesis of Michael Warner, "Introduction: Fear of a Queer Planet," *Social Text* 29 (1991): 3–17. See also George L. Mosse, *Nationalism and Sexuality: Middle-Class Morality and Sexual Norms in Modern Europe* (Madison: University of Wisconsin Press, 1985); and the introduction to *Nationalisms and Sexualities*, ed. Andrew Parker, Mary Parker, Russo, Doris Sommer, and Patricia Yaeger (New York: Routledge, 1991). Parallels between the gay ghetto and other dissident subcultures may be extrapolated from James C. Scott, *Domination and the Arts of Resistance* (New Haven: Yale University Press, 1990), chap. 5. Although William Burroughs once proposed the establishment of a gay state analogous to Israel, he later abandoned the idea. He suggested instead organizations within existing states modeled after the Chinese tongs, which he called Gay Protection patrols, or GPs (after San Francisco's groups to protect gays against street violence). However, the GPs would also provide services to their members: assistance in finding employment and housing, legal advice and assistance, medical aid, protection from extortion, and meeting and recreational facilities. Most of these services have come to be offered in a decentralized manner by the gay communities of large U.S. cities, including orienta-

therefore in the situation of constituting themselves as a political community that is dispersed throughout society, fighting homophobia wherever it occurs.

The contemporary lesbian and gay movement since Stonewall has made living one's life as an openly gay or lesbian person a criterion of "liberation." The debate between lesbian and gay separatism and integration (indeed, including lesbian separatism within the lesbian/gay separatist position) has also been continuous since then. But should such a life be lived in as much isolation from nongay society as possible (which would allow, it is said, for a greater richness of personal and communal development), or should gays and lesbians integrate themselves *as gays* and *as lesbians* (forcibly, or using legal means if feasible) into the warp and woof of the fabric of the society in which they live? An exemplary statement of the first of these positions appears in Howard Brookner's film *Burroughs,* where William Burroughs argues the case for a gay state where gays in the diaspora will always be able to count on having a homeland; a statement of the second position lies in AIDS activist Larry Kramer's Arendtian parallels between Jewish and gay male political experience:

---

tion sessions for lesbians and gay men who have just migrated from the hinterlands. Burroughs sees the necessity for these kinds of organizations in even the smallest towns nationwide. Moreover, it may be true, as Dennis Altman argued in 1985, that "the past decade and a half has seen the creation of a gay and lesbian 'nation,' much as nineteenth-century Europe saw the creation of Czech and Roumanian 'nations.' To be gay has taken on meanings that go far beyond sexual and affectional preference, binding us through a whole set of communal, religious, political and social activities with other gays." See William S. Burroughs, "Thoughts on a Gay State," in *Gay Spirit: Myth and Meaning*, ed. Mark Thompson (New York: St. Martin's Press, 1987), 20–24,

> For a while, San Francisco was the gays' Israel. For decades, gays migrated there, and in time they attained great power in the political structure of that city. No mayor there would consider *not* consulting with gay leaders. And this gay power was sufficient to keep most local heterosexual opposition in check. Tragically, with the devastation of AIDS, gay power in San Francisco has waned considerably: Many of the leaders have died.
>
> We don't have Zionism as a hopeful haven from the world's hatred of us. And, as Arendt pointed out, Zionism's solution was not one of fighting anti-Semitism on its own ground, that is, wherever it existed, but to escape it.
>
> As Arendt wrote to support her thesis: "The simple truth is that Jews will have to fight anti-Semitism everywhere or else be exterminated everywhere."[10]

A most eloquent statement of the lesbian separatist position has been made by Marilyn Frye, but even she discovers conditions of possibility for a community of both lesbians and gay men, to the extent that sexism among gay men subsides: "If there is hope for a coordination of the efforts and insights of lesbian feminists and gay men, it is . . . when we are working from chosen foundations in our different differences."[11]

---

and Dennis Altman, "What Price Gay Nationalism?" in Thompson, *Gay Spirit*, 16–19, at 18–19.

10. Larry Kramer, *Reports from the Holocaust: The Making of an AIDS Activist* (New York: St. Martin's Press, 1989), 254, 257.

11. Marilyn Frye, *The Politics of Reality* (Freedom, Calif.: Crossing Press, 1983), 128–51, at 150.

From Lifestyle to Community

The concept of lifestyle is a characteristic way through which, in modern times, individuals come to understand themselves and their relations with others, as well as their life course and choices; it is also a principal site at which we have all come to be governed. The problematization of their own lifestyle (indeed, more broadly, their way of life) has been based upon a conscious imperative among lesbians and gay men to invent the self and ways of relating to others. In spite of the historical and cross-cultural prevalence of homosexuality, lesbians and gay men must create a self out of (or despite) the heterosexual self that is culturally given to them (and, because of the suppression and falsification of the historical record, imposed upon them as inevitable).[12] They must invent ways of relating to each other because there are no ready-made cultural or historical models or formulas for erotic same-sex relationships, as there are for different-sex erotic relationships. They must do so, further, in a cultural environment of extreme prejudice, which denies their existence outright or, at best, allows them to exist by "passing"—adopting a heterosexual persona or, if

12. The best analysis of the suppression, and even falsification, of historical data on homosexuality remains John Boswell, *Christianity, Social Tolerance, and Homosexuality: Gay People in Western Europe from the Beginning of the Christian Era to the Fourteenth Century* (Chicago: University of Chicago Press, 1980); see particularly the overview of the problem on 17–22. For example, on 20–21 he writes: "Sometimes their anxiety to reinterpret or disguise accounts of homosexuality has induced translators to inject wholly new concepts into texts, as when the translators of a Hittite law apparently regulating homosexual marriage insert words which completely alter its meaning or when Graves 'translates' a nonexistent clause in Suetonius to suggest that a law prohibits homosexual acts."

they are openly gay or lesbian, by adopting a mode of relating to each other that mimics heterosexual "couples." Thus, contemporary gay men and lesbians live in a situation where, because of their sexual and affectional attractions, they must create relationships and networks of relations with each other against the void in which they have historically and culturally found themselves.

Lesbians and gay men virtually invent a way of life through which they create and re-create the self continually within sexual-affectional relationships, which differ in kind and vary in intensity. These relationships and the way of life that they contribute to creating have, of course, nothing to do with any intrinsic qualities of homosexuals. Rather, they grow out of the lack of cultural models or historical traditions for contemporary lesbians and gay men to fall back upon and use to inform their relationships. Contemporary lesbian and gay existence involves, therefore, the creation of a way of life—understood as a primary means of creating one's own self in and through one's relations with others. Indeed, the extreme creativity that must be exercised by lesbians and gay men just to live day to day, not to mention flourish, cannot be overemphasized. It is the possibility of a lesbian and gay way of life that maps out the contemporary battlegrounds for lesbian and gay existence: the right to make one's own erotic choices, the freeing of a space for a lesbian and gay relational culture that arises out of such erotic choices, and the objectification of these as value, guiding the production and the institutionalization of knowledge. All these presuppose, for their realization, the emergence of a lesbian and gay way of life more encompassing than a lifestyle—what I call an ethos.

However, in the modern age power has come to be exercised as biopower; as the object of government, the processes of life are now mastered through the control of how the individual lives and of how the individual manages his or her own life in relations with others. Techniques of government, broadly understood, are the more or less deliberate and institutionally organized exercise of power over individuals and collectivities; they involve, as well, the capacity to set the framework within which individuals themselves shape their own conduct and produce their own individuality. These techniques ultimately tend to focus upon fostering or disallowing various elements of one's lifestyle.[13]

Now, as the concept of a lifestyle has become in modern times an object for government, it has concomitantly become a primary way through which people generally understand and identify themselves to others. That is, lifestyle makes up the part of one's life that is the principal object of self-reflection and self-creation (what I have called "ethical self-constitution"—working on oneself to create that self as a sub-

13. The government of lifestyle has historically been an important strategy in both the United States and the former Soviet Union. For example, one motive for such governing in the United States was the "Americanization" of immigrants through programs to train them in the "American way of life"; similarly, the Bolsheviks gave themselves the task of creating the new Communist Man. The consequences in both societies were that the "individual's 'private' life and 'personal' activities were now matters of the well-being of the population: they entered into a calculus of social costs and needed to be governed." Keith Gandal and Stephen Kotkin, "Governing Work and Social Life in the U.S.A. and U.S.S.R.," *History of the Present* 1 (February 1985): 4–14.

ject of one's actions). The concept of one's lifestyle in contemporary Western societies comes to overshadow, even as it incorporates, more traditional sources of identity, such as race, religion, ethnicity, class, and occupation in people's self-understanding; indeed, in recent years it has become a general category of sociological and even epidemiological analysis.[14] Further, the modern self is obliged, not by law but within the sphere of consumption and through a market of expertise, to construct a life by choosing among alternative conducts, values, and aspirations; to understand one's own life through the outcomes of such choices; and then to account for one's life in terms of the reasons for one's choices.[15] Thus, to the extent that lesbians and gays understand themselves as living a specific lifestyle, they participate in a way of thinking about themselves that is at once characteristic of modernity and that is also a principal modality through which power has come to be exercised over all of us.

However, the concept of lifestyle is not quite adequate as descriptive of or as a hermeneutic approach to the self-understanding involved in lesbian and gay existence, or as a basis for (collective) self-reflection.

---

14. See, for example, Michael E. Sobel, *Lifestyle and Social Structure: Concepts, Definitions, Analyses* (New York: Academic Press, 1981); Mike Featherstone, "Lifestyle and Consumer Culture," *Theory, Culture, and Society* 4 (1987): 55–70; and Bryan S. Turner, *Status* (Minneapolis: University of Minnesota Press, 1988), chap. 4. For lifestyle as a category of epidemiological analysis, and its failure (owing to its stereotypical character) to account for AIDS etiology, see Gerald M. Oppenheimer, "In the Eye of the Storm: The Epidemiological Construction of AIDS," in *AIDS: The Burdens of History*, ed. Elizabeth Fee and Daniel M. Fox (Berkeley and Los Angeles: University of California Press, 1988), 267–300.

15. Nikolas Rose, *Governing the Soul: The Shaping of the Private Self* (London and New York: Routledge, 1990), 227.

Lifestyle implies consumerism, where the individual "speaks not only with his clothes, but with his home, furnishings, decoration, car and other activities which are to be read and classified in terms of the presence or absence of taste," which is itself an embodiment of social status (again, reflecting but surpassing class, gender, ethnicity, region, and even political ideology).[16] The way of life of lesbian and gay people, on the contrary, is much more a function of an ascetic *becoming* lesbian or gay through a learning approach to life in the context of a lesbian or gay community. Here, working on the self—one's *life itself,* according to criteria specific to the way one lives it through the relationships that constitute that community—is the object of ethico-aesthetic work, rather than its material accoutrements as determined through individualistic criteria. (To be sure, the concept of an *ascetic* becoming needs to be differentiated from the "asceticism" our culture inherited from Christianity, which involves the devaluing of erotic desire and the mortification of the flesh. Lesbians and gay men, rather, participate in the "self-help" or self-shaping techniques, discourses, and institutions of the lesbian and gay community through which one forms oneself as an ethical subject of one's own actions. This lesbian and gay erotic ascesis is the basis for their ethos.)

A lifestyle, therefore, can have a largely evanescent quality, being a product of individual fashion or whim—"Today there is no fashion: there are only *fashions*. 'No rules, only choices.' 'Everyone can be

16. Featherstone, "Lifestyle," 59, 64.

anyone—.' "[17] The fact that homoerotic practices are transmitted from generation to generation in spite of familial and cultural suppression suggests something like a sexual orientation or predisposition. However, the fact that contemporary lesbian and gay people can adapt to radically changing circumstances and treatment of them within a given society (e.g., through sexual codes and secret societies) suggests that survival is made possible through something collective that is distinct from a mere lifestyle. (The anthropologist Gilbert Herdt, for example, has identified the era of AIDS, as well as the development of the lesbian and gay community, as ushering in "for the first time an institutionalized process of initiating and socializing [lesbian and gay] youths."[18]

However, a lifestyle can also be a category for the analysis of—and indeed can designate the suppression of—individuality within the context of a collectivity with shared values to which the individual is held accountable. I am reminded of some New Left writers' suggestions to fashion one's life into a vehicle for political transformation, a kind of politically correct lifestyle, and of a recent proposal by gay male writers for a new gay lifestyle, organized around a "Self-Policing Social Code," because the present gay lifestyle is "unworkable . . . diminish[es] the quality of gay life, and make[s] us look bad to straights . . . [because it is] devoid of the values that straight society, with such good

17. Ibid., 55 (emphasis in original).

18. Gilbert Herdt, "Coming Out as a Rite of Passage: A Chicago Study," in *Gay Culture in America: Essays from the Field*, ed. Gilbert Herdt (Boston: Beacon Press, 1991), 34.

reason, respects."[19] Their social code would be enforced through gay social censure—by the gay victim of and the gay witness to "gay misbehavior." I reproduce it here to demonstrate how moral discourse about lifestyle has arisen within the lesbian and gay community, but also to show how its content, shaped as it is by the desire to conform to existing heterosexist norms rather than to create lesbian and gay criteria for existence, results in the untenable paradox of either its own abstract moralism or what it suggests as the alternative, gay nihilism. Nevertheless, circulation and debate about such moral or normative concerns within the lesbian and gay community allows individuals to use codal elements to shape their own behavior—ethics—as I discuss in the context of the emergence of an ethos.

I have been arguing, therefore, that sexual orientation, since it is a term derived as a response to a psychiatric diagnosis of homosexuality as illness, is not adequate to describe the contemporary lesbian and gay condition. Likewise, the concept of lifestyle is inadequate to describe how lesbians and gay men think of themselves in relation to each other (as sharing a lifestyle), because there is nothing about lesbian and gay existence that makes lifestyle uniquely informative about it or empowering. Furthermore, there are, empirically, many different ways of living as gay or lesbian—lipstick/fashion dyke, lesbian feminist, leatherfolk, queer, butch/femme, gay Republican, the

---

19. Marshall Kirk and Hunter Madsen, *After the Ball: How America Will Conquer Its Fear and Hatred of Gays in the '90s* (New York: Doubleday, 1989), 305.

Figure 4. A Self-Policing Social Code

Rules for Relations with Straights

I Won't Have Sex in Public Places.

I Won't Make Passes at Straight Acquaintances, or at Strangers Who Might Not Be Gay.

Wherever Possible and Sensible, I Will Come Out—Gracefully.

I Will Make an Effort, When Among Straights, Not to Live Down to Gay Stereotypes.

I Won't Talk Gay Sex and Gay Raunch in Public.

If I'm a Pederast or a Sadomasochist, I'll Keep It Under Wraps, and Out of Gay Pride Marches.

If I'm Transvestite, However Glamorous, I'll Graciously Decline Invitations to Model Lingerie for "Oprah" or "Donahue."

Rules for Relations with Other Gays

I Won't Lie.

I Won't Cheat on My Lover—or with Someone Else's.

I'll Encourage Other Gays to Come Out, But Never Expose Them Against Their Will.

Tested or Otherwise, I'll Practice Safe Sex.

I'll Contribute Money in Meaningful Amounts to the Gay Cause.

I Will Not Speak Scornfully or Cruelly of Another's Age, Looks, Clothing, or Social Class, in Bars or Elsewhere, Lest I Reveal My Own Insecurities.

When Forced to Reject a Suitor, I Will Do So Firmly but Kindly.

I'll Drop My Search for Mr. Right and Settle for What's Realistic.

I Won't Re-Enact Straight Oppression by Name-Calling and Shouting Down Gays Whose Opinions Don't Square with Mine.

Rules for Relations with Yourself

I'll Stop Trying to Be Eighteen Forever and Act My Age; I Won't Punish Myself for Being What I Am.

I Won't Have More Than Two Alcoholic Drinks a Day; I Won't Use Street Drugs at All.

I'll Get a Stable, Productive Job and Become a Member of the Wider Community Beyond the Gay Ghetto.

I'll Live for Something Meaningful Beyond Myself.

When Confronted by Real Problems, I'll Listen to Common Sense, Not Emotion.

I Will Not Condone Sexual Practices I Think Harmful to Individuals or to the Community Just Because They're Homosexual.

I'll Start Making Some Value Judgments.

SOURCE: From Marshall Kirk and Hunter Madsen, *After the Ball: How America Will Conquer Its Fear and Hatred of Gays in the 1990s*, 360. Copyright © 1989 by Marshall Kirk and Hunter Madsen. Used by permission of Doubleday, a division of Bantam Doubleday Publishing Group, Inc.

Hannah Arendt Lesbian Peace Patrol of Western Massachusetts. These are but a few of many different lesbian and gay male lifestyles.

Subculture and Community

Does lesbian and gay subculture and community provide a basis for hermeneutic description of, or self-reflection upon, lesbian and gay existence? The lesbian philosopher Sarah Lucia Hoagland, acknowledging the influence of another lesbian philosopher, Julia Penelope, makes a distinction between subculture and community. "A lesbian subculture is a group we become part of automatically by declaring ourselves lesbian—but a group 'wholly defined in negative terms by an external, hostile culture that sees us as deviates from their 'norm.' "[20] Further, the bonds formed among people in such a subculture that struggles against oppression are better conceived as alliances; the bonds will not necessarily endure beyond the immediate struggle. On the other hand, membership in a lesbian and gay community (Hoagland, as a separatist, is writing of lesbian community) is voluntary. She continues:

> If we are to form an enduring community it will not be on the basis of outside threats. Further, it will not be on the basis of a rich tradition nor of what we find here (though we do have crone-ology). If we are to form an empowering community, it will be on the basis of the values we believe we can enact here: what we bring, what we

20. Sarah Lucia Hoagland, *Lesbian Ethics: Toward New Value* (Palo Alto, Calif.: Institute for Lesbian Studies, 1988), 146.

> work to leave behind, and what we develop as we engage each other. If we are to transform subculture into community, it will be on the basis of what we create, not what we find. And attempts to control each other won't hold us together; instead, they actually undermine our ability, particularly our moral agency. (155)

Thus, from this perspective, subculture is a negative community, existing as a reaction to a common threat, or, as in the case of what has been called the gay ghetto, to provide cultural nourishment to people who are aliens in the larger culture. The kind of community that Hoagland conceptualizes for lesbians, however, does not yet exist; they represent themselves in writing more commonly as making up commun*ities* with shared affinities and working alliances among them.[21] Further, to the extent that such a concept of community implies sharing primary-group membership (e.g., intimate friendships, living arrangements), there is, arguably, something more like an alliance between gay men and lesbians through the organizations and publications that they have formed for political expediency (one such organization, the Human Rights Campaign Fund, is one of the largest political action committees in the United States). In the relational dimension of everyday life,

---

21. The theory of "identity politics," that individuals have crosscutting identities (woman, Native American, lesbian, etc.) that structure both their subjective social experience and their loyalties to others, also suggests limits on the possibility of "community" between lesbians and gay men. For theoretical discussions of identity politics, see Shane Phelan, *Identity Politics: Lesbian Feminism and the Limits of Community* (Philadelphia: Temple University Press, 1989); and Diana Fuss, *Essentially Speaking: Feminism, Nature, and Difference* (London and New York: Routledge, 1989), chap. 4.

there is still a delicate balance between separatism and friendship involving lesbians and gay men (this is even more the case in urban areas where the lesbian and gay community has become more elaborated).

However, despite this caveat, there is an ongoing creation of a common lesbian and gay male culture that includes the construction of a history, an anthropology, and, more generally, a scholarly and public discourse about lesbian and gay existence (besides Hoagland's "crone-ology").[22] And there are other indicators of the existence of community between lesbians and gay men: concentration in space (based on residence, but also through participation in community institutions); learned and shared norms; institutional completeness within the community serving both lesbians and gay men (including basic social services—health services, bookstores, religious organizations, travel agencies, charities, political clubs); collective action (street demonstrations, lesbian and gay pride marches, lobbying efforts); a sense of a shared history; and commitments that go beyond private life and into public endeavors (to cite but two examples: the election of African American mayors in New York, Chicago, and Philadelphia has been attributed by voting-behavior specialists to pivotal lesbian and gay political mobilization and voting; and a number of U.S.

---

22. There are lesbian and gay book series at Columbia University Press, NAL, St. Martin's, and several exclusively lesbian and gay presses; a lesbian and gay studies center at the City University of New York, as well as many academic programs elsewhere; several national academic conferences—three at Yale, one each at Harvard, Rutgers, and Iowa—and plans for more; yearly national lesbian and gay writers' conferences and award competitions; and numerous joint lesbian/gay publications. Moreover, 1991 saw the founding of a North American lesbian and gay studies association.

cities and states have openly lesbian or gay elected officials).[23] Finally, and also following Hoagland, membership in this community is a consequence of voluntary participation (joining organizations, financially supporting political initiatives, etc.). Inversely, the community is not held together through laws, or even informally through a self-policing social code; attempts by lesbians and gays to "try to control each other," especially by excluding people whose erotic-object choice is the same sex but who are different in other ways (into S/M, involved in cross-generational relationships, do drag, etc.) have been notoriously divisive and unsuccessful. Both lesbians and gay men remain ambivalent about the desirability of *communitas*, the experience on a subjective level of undifferentiated harmony; this is partially due, no doubt, to their own prior experience of heterosexist community, with its homophobia and sexism from which many of them fled.

Nevertheless, by standard sociological indicators, lesbian and gay community exists, especially in the urban areas to which lesbians and gay men have most often fled. What is most important about it, though, is not *communitas,* unanimity of fellow feeling (which is not necessary to serve the purpose the community does in fact serve, and to which I shall return), but that this sociologic community *does* facilitate the creation of what Hoagland variously calls moral agency and

---

23. These "technical social science" indexes of community are from Stephen O. Murray, "Components of Gay Community in San Francisco" in *Gay Culture*, ed. Herdt, 113–16. The research on gay and lesbian voting behavior is being led by Robert W. Bailey of Rutgers University and the Gay and Lesbian Caucus for Political Science.

lesbian be-ing, that is, the creation of a specific kind of subjectivity. This distinctive lesbian and gay subjectivity requires an appropriate descriptive category. This is so because lesbian and gay people are "everywhere" since they have blood ties with nongay people, and because of the particular kind of community they form with each other. It is territorial, but also nonterritorial, the latter forming a public sphere (writing, media, community centers, public/town meetings, organizations and their leadership, and the formation of a lesbian and gay *public*). The descriptive category that most closely approximates what lesbian and gay existence is today is ethos: the creation of ethical agency within and through a lesbian and gay community. This ethos is lived and acted beyond the community, carried into the larger world as ethics, even though it depends upon the community and its public sphere for its conditions of possibility.

The Emergence of a Lesbian and Gay Ethos

The condition of existence for community is coming out. This involves more than the narrow meaning usually attributed to it as a single act whereby an individual declares his or her identity as homosexual, gay, or lesbian to family, friends, or coworkers who previously assumed the person to be nongay. As it has been conceptualized here, coming out is a lifelong process of *becoming* lesbian or gay. As such, it is a practical creation of the self that involves working on a specific aspect of oneself—one's gay or lesbian sexuality, using external sources of authority as guidance for such a work on oneself, deploying specific techniques—

objective practices through which one forms oneself and makes oneself appear to others, and fashioning oneself toward a goal to which one aspires. If coming out is a condition for the existence of community, then that community becomes a condition of possibility for a lesbian and gay ethos—being able to live one's life *as* a lesbian or *as* a gay man or *as* a gay woman, which is the goal of the coming-out process.

Through all of these components of coming out, one enters into a specific kind of discourse and practices about what it means to be lesbian or gay, which the existence of community has made possible and through which one voluntarily forms oneself as an ethical subject in relation to the values of that community. To be sure, coming out is a recognition of one's homoeroticism as a basic element of one's being; how one acts upon that recognition (camouflaging it, participating in community institutions in order to shape one's sexuality, entering conversion therapy) is a matter of choice.

Now, historically, the concept of ethos has not always been applied in this erotic sense. It is erotic among lesbian and gay people because, in the context of cultural domination and subjection, the part of themselves that they have had to pay most attention to ethically, and that hence centers the way they live their lives, is their sexuality and their erotic relationships. Etymologically, "ethos" connotes something deeply embedded in one's existence—indeed, for the Stoics it was the *source* of behavior—that, while learned, is not based upon adherence to a belief system (even though it may be a conscious practice) but is habitual.[24] For example, in Plato's *Phaedo* (82b), "Happiest are those who have cultivated the goodness of an ordinary citizen [the political excellences] which is acquired by habit and practice, without the help of philosophy and reason." Similar usages are found in Thucydides, Sophocles, Aeschylus, and in Aristotle, where ethos is the outcome of moral rather than intellective understandings. Nietzsche associated ethos with the stylizing of one's behavior, which Michel Foucault later took up as an "aesthetics of existence."[25] Max Weber, in his introduction to *The Protestant Ethic and the Spirit of Capitalism*, conceptualizes ethos as the "spirit" of an economic system; Protestantism's worldly ascetism gave rise to, in his view, the ethos of capitalism.[26] Martin Heidegger, who associated ethos with "poetical dwelling," wrote: "The tragedies of Sophocles preserve the *ethos* in their sagas more primordially than Aristotle's lectures on 'ethics,' " and he credits Hölderlin with reclaiming the tragedians' conception of ethos as a poetical dwelling place, the touchstone for his own notion of authentic existence, which requires poetical thinking and dwelling.[27] Heidegger relies upon the poetical

---

24. I thank Dante Germino for his assistance in documenting for me the Greek etymology of "ethos." The translation from Plato is his.

25. "The idea of a morality as obedience to a code of rules is now disappearing, has already disappeared. To this absence of a morality, one responds, or must respond, with a research which is that of an aesthetics of existence." Michel Foucault, "An Aesthetics of Existence," in *Foucault Live*, trans. John Johnston, ed. Sylvere Lotringer (New York: Semiotexte, 1989), 311.

26. Trans. Talcott Parsons (1930, New York: Charles Scribner's Sons, 1958), 27.

27. Cited in Calvin O. Schrag, *Communicative Praxis and the Space of Subjectivity* (Bloomington: Indiana University Press, 1986), 210. My discussion of ethos is informed by Schrag's excellent chapter "Ethos, Ethics, and a New Humanism."

somewhat as a reaction, it appears, to what he perceived as modern philosophy's "degradation" of ethos into ethics having its origin in an atomistic moral subject possessing values as "personality traits." Ethos, for him, "denotes not mere norms but mores, based on freely accepted obligations and traditions; it is that which concerns free behavior and attitudes, the shaping of man's historical being, the *ethos* which under the influence of morality was later degraded to the ethical."[28]

Therefore, just as ethos needs to be understood apart from its reduction by social science to the individual as a carrier of moral interests and values, so it also needs to be understood apart from mere aestheticism—that which finds expression in the notion of a homosexual sensibility that Susan Sontag and others emblematized as "camp": "a private code, a badge of identity even . . . the consistently aesthetic experience of the world . . . a victory of 'style' over 'content,' 'aesthetics' over 'morality,' of irony over tragedy."[29] Even though ethos incorporates such stylized comportment, it is at the same time an ethico-political category that, as a living ethical practice that gives rise to responsibilities while being voluntary and contingent, avoids the dualism of abstract normativism (with its moral yardsticks, such as the self-policing gay social code) and moral relativism or nihilism. Rather, ethos is a

---

28. Martin Heidegger, *An Introduction to Metaphysics*, trans. Ralph Manheim (1959; Garden City, N.Y.: Doubleday, 1961), 13 (emphasis in original).

29. Susan Sontag, "Notes on 'Camp,'" in *Against Interpretation and Other Essays* (New York: Dell, 1966), 275, 287.

type of existence that is the consequence of coming out—understood as the process of entering into and creating oneself through the field of relationships that constitutes the lesbian and gay community. From this process of self-creation arise *freely chosen* responsibilities, conceptions of what is proper and fitting, that get constituted as selfhood, as what it means to be lesbian and gay.

Yet this ethos is *historical* in both a biographical and a communal sense. As a type of subjectivity, formed through coming out into the relationships that constitute community, its formation does not have an end point for the individual but continues throughout life. At the same time, individuals, through their self-constitution and crafting of an ethos, preserve, amend, reassess, and displace elements of this ethos: a lesbian and gay ethos is historically constructed and historically changing. For example, such people as Jean Genet, Quentin Crisp, and Gertrude Stein lived a homosexual ethos (if it can even be called that—they invented their ways of living without participation in a lesbian or gay community, which did not yet exist) of defiant self-assertion (Genet), flaunting (Crisp), and cosmopolitan bohemianism (Stein). Elements of their ethos are preserved in that of today's lesbians and gay men—in the reclaiming of them as lesbian and gay historical predecessors, through the recognition of "outsider" status in the context of continuing heterosexism and the will to develop a way of life that does not mimic its norms—to be militantly "queer," and through participation, trans-locally and trans-nationally in what has been called lesbian and gay gesellschaft, or the "queer nation."[30]

Finally, ethos does more than just inform politics. It *is* political in a fundamental way. As the development of one's ethical agency through entering into the discourse of what it means to be lesbian or gay in the practice of coming out, ethos is at the same time the development of what Plato called "the political excellences." Since ethos is a sexual and relational way of living shared with others by virtue of one's participation in—indeed, creation of oneself through—the lesbian and gay community, the morale and destiny of that community is at stake in being able to live one's own ethos. Thus, in the formation of an ethos, the question posed earlier—"How shall I live?"—becomes inextricably connected to "How shall we live?" The stake one has in the morale and destiny of the local lesbian and gay community (the context that makes one's "self" possible) becomes a stake in civic involvement in wider socio-historical existence in all of its aspects as they affect one's ability to come out and live a lesbian and gay ethos—particularly in the wider lesbian and gay culture that exists by virtue of national and international lesbian and gay communit*ies*, the totality of which is gesellschaft. (That is why we should be concerned about racism, sexism, and ageism within the lesbian and gay community. All these affect the morale of the community and hence one's ability to live within it, as well as the possibility that those so disempowered will come out into the lesbian and gay community.)

---

30. For a discussion of gay gemeinschaft and gesellschaft see Herdt, *Gay Culture*, 11–12.

An ethos, then, while formed in community, is enacted throughout the fabric of everyday life. It is not enacted only in relations with other lesbian and gay people, or just in gay neighborhoods. As the formation of an attitude, an *ethic,* uniting character and behavior, ethos relates lesbian and gay people to each other in a gesellschaft beyond their local gay gemeinschaft. Indeed, it is an attitude—that of the so-called openly gay man or avowed lesbian—that they carry into whatever social environment they happen to be in and, importantly, into whatever position of sociocultural power or authority they occupy. This attitude involves giving one's life distinctive form through a relation to oneself in which one is inventing oneself, coming out, through a relation to others where one is recognized and appreciated through the style one gives to one's existence (as one lesbian describes herself, "A Fully Revolting Hag in the Department of Philosophy," mischievously alluding to the importance of the role model for the status of truth in lesbian and gay politics).[31] But this ethical attitude is also a relation to the present, where, in one's own way and through one's own life, one confronts and displaces compulsory heterosexuality. Unlike the self-policing social code that prescribes moral rules of behavior, a lesbian and gay ethos emerges not so much from moral as from existential criteria—the discourse of lived experi-

31. This lesbian is Claudia Card, as she describes herself in her contributor's biography in *Lesbian Philosophies and Cultures*, ed. Jeffner Allen (Albany: State University of New York Press, 1990), 407. For analysis of role models along lines I have adumbrated, see Anita L. Allen, "The Role Model Argument and Faculty Diversity," *The Philosophical Forum* 24 (1–3) (1992–93): 267–81.

ence of lesbians and gay men about the diverse meanings of what it means to be lesbian and gay in the present moment. And more than the criteria of whether lesbians and gay men should be assimilationist or separatist, or whether individual adherence to a liberal or a conservative political ideology will advance "the cause," what is a *distinctive* criterion of existence is a lesbian and gay ethos, understood both as coming out and as integrating one's homoerotic relationships within all of one's social relationships. Therefore, an emergent lesbian and gay ethos would consist in an ethico-political choice. This would not involve disciplining others and oneself on behalf of a code of behavior. The aim, rather, would be to stylize one's own existence toward the elaboration of selfhood as lesbian or gay; to gain recognition by others as such; and, also as such, *publicly* (in the dual meaning of being socially visible and of moving into the public/political realm) to introduce a change in, undermining, the order of compulsory heterosexuality.

Ethos, Knowledge, and Politics

The concept of coming out can be crystallized into three axes of experience, corresponding to the three "moments" of politics analyzed throughout this book. First is the axis of subjectivity—one's relation to oneself—in coming out to oneself through one's erotic relationships; erotics involves practices that link individual to collective identity from which a social movement comes into existence. Second, there is coming out to others socially (in family, occupation, and other social interactions), corresponding to the axis of experience that consists in exercising and submitting to power in relations that engage the legal system and other institutions, which corresponds to the second moment of politics—the assertion of lesbian and gay rights. Finally, there is coming out in one's imagination or understanding of the world *the way it is lived as a lesbian or gay person* (as distinct from having a subjected or "colonized" understanding because of a culture that privileges heterosexuality). The creation, by lesbians and gays themselves, of the "truth about homosexuality" corresponds to that moment of politics where compulsory heterosexuality is displaced in the order of knowledge. This truth then becomes integrated into the knowledge of human actuality. It corresponds to the axis of experience that is one's relation to what is established as true—and to how it is established—in the world in which one lives. Coming out is a lifelong process, more than an initial realization, a public assertion that one is lesbian or gay, or a later adaptation to the historically changing norms of the lesbian and gay community. It is, rather, the continuous process of individual and collective empowerment in the historical context of heterosexist domination and homophobic subjection, even though its ultimate goal may be a world in which same-sex erotics is integrated into psyche and society and in which coming out is no longer necessary. But as a process of empowerment, the creation of an ethos through coming out is integral to the production of truth. This involves both the truth claims of the discourse about sexuality and the power effects of such discourse.

An ethos of lesbian and gay existence is a source

for the production of truth.[32] By "truth," I mean, again, procedures for producing statements to the effect (following Wittgenstein) "this is how things are" and for institutionalizing both them as knowledge and people who "tell the truth." In this case, it is procedures for producing, regulating, distributing, and circulating statements about homoeroticism historically and about the experience of it as lesbian or gay today. Indeed, it is ethos, as coming out in recognition of and in the context of a lesbian and gay community, that motivates the production of truth. This happens in order to counter the representation of homosexuality and lesbian and gay existence by its enemies, but also because, as Nietzsche said, "It is our needs that interpret the world."[33] A way of life produces knowledge needed in order to exist in the world at a particular historical moment. This ethos necessitates the production of knowledge, understood not just as theory, but including practical guides to and reflections upon living—such as self-help manuals (concerning medicine, the law, relationships, etc.), fiction, autobiography and biography, and scientific research. This knowledge is both a truth in visibility (that destroys stereotypes) and a *technē*, broader than skill or technology, that is the objectification of the values of the community, the putting to work of its being and stabilizing it in something present (to draw a gloss on Heidegger).[34] Such knowledge allows the community collec-

32. Ludwig Wittgenstein, *Philosophical Investigations,* trans. G.E.M. Anscombe (Oxford: Basil Blackwell, 1968), 52.

33. Friedrich Nietzsche, *The Will to Power*, trans. Walter Kaufmann and R. J. Hollingdale, ed. Walter Kaufmann (New York: Random House/Vintage Books, 1967), section 481.

34. Heidegger, *An Introduction to Metaphysics*, 133–34. Earlier in the book (13–14), Heidegger states that *technē* "denotes neither art nor technology but a knowledge, the ability to plan and organize freely, to

tively (and the individuals within it) to exercise power through which heterosexism can be undermined and homophobia can be prevented or discredited.[35] This knowledge consists of a history of the present constructed from those contents of the past that have been deliberately suppressed or disguised within a methodological privileging of heterosexuality, combined with the discourse of lived experience about contemporary lesbian and gay existence by the participants themselves. This is a kind of knowledge production that, even when institutionalized through the university, mass media, writing, and the state (thereby giving it broader legitimation and empowering lesbians and gay people), is not centralized within these established institutions for the production and distribution of knowledge. This is the case even though a political struggle is now under way within them concerning its status as lesbian and gay studies (as was previously the case with women's studies, for example).[36]

---

master institutions (cf. Plato's *Phaedrus*). *Technē* is creating, building in the sense of a deliberate pro-ducing." See also Michel Foucault's discussion of the ancient *technē tou biou*—knowledge, practices, and institutions for the cultivation of the self—the theme of the third volume of his history of sexuality. In interviews, he also stated his belief that the development of such a *technē*, an art of living, was integral to contemporary lesbian and gay existence (and, I would add, to the creation of an ethos that links ethical agency with political action). See Michel Foucault, *The History of Sexuality*, vol. 3, *The Care of the Self*, trans. Robert Hurley (New York: Pantheon Books, 1986), 43–45, 88–92; and Bob Gallagher and Alexander Wilson, "Michel Foucault, an Interview: Sex, Power, and the Politics of Identity," *The Advocate*, no. 400 (August 7, 1984): 26–30, 58.

35. Examples would include the now nearly universally promulgated safer-sex guidelines, developed by gay men to maintain, in the face of AIDS, the kinds of relationships in which they were engaging, as well as lesbian insemination and the redefinition of family that it (with the help of styles of gay male relationships) is eliciting.

36. Thus there is a permanent tension between the "unqualified" character of this knowledge (it is either "interested"—not objective or

To be sure, the production of truth is not to be confused with the creation of value. The lesbian and gay movement has created value from erotic experience, problematizing, transforming, and inventing the possibility for experience. Such value is lived as an ethos and it is that ethos that affects what shall become an object for knowledge in our society. And it is in this manner that lesbians and gay people significantly affect the reality in which all people live, both because truth is a qualification through which power can be exercised, and because of power's role in the shaping of subjectivity. It is not "value relativism" or "cultural diversity" that is at stake here. What is at stake are the historically specific procedures through which, in our culture, something becomes an object for knowledge and how that knowledge is institutionalized, and the capacity of a dominated group to affect those procedures that contribute to its domination (e.g., funding or not funding biomedical research for treating and eliminating sexually transmitted diseases, or developing school curricula on homosexuality and gay and lesbian relationships). A lesbian and gay ethos challenges the historical installation of sexuality into a regime of truth by shifting the domain of behaviors that have constituted "the sexual" away from intelligibility through truth claims about what sexuality *is* based solely upon procreation and sexual dimorphism and

---

sufficiently distanced from subjective experience—or it is not always the product of scientific inquiry or not adequately theorized) and the drive toward codification by, for example, lesbian and gay studies programs and by the professionalization of lesbian and gay activists when they strive to cooperate with established institutions in order to change those institutions' policies.

complementarity toward intelligibility as individual choice and creation. Coming out and constitution and elaboration of oneself in erotic relations with others is the ethos—the normative transformation that lesbians and gays effect in everyday life—from which their politics springs.

Gay and Lesbian Politics and a New Ethic

A gay and lesbian ethos serves as a condition of possibility for politics (understood as creating and as placing limits upon what is conceived as political). In addition to being a preeminently *political* experience, coming out marks at once a redefinition of the self, a rite of passage in one's relationships with others and an act of *volition.* As the creation of agency, the self appears and becomes—through working on an ethical substance (one's sexuality), through new, nonheterosexist sources of authority (*now* the lesbian and gay community), through specific erotico-social practices that one engages in (practices through which sexuality is integrated into, rather than being a "parenthesis" within, everyday life) with the goal of living a lesbian or gay way of life, or ethos.

As part of such a process of becoming, one does not come out passively or accidentally. Thus one can never really be "outed" by another, except in the very narrow sense of exposing sexual behavior that had been kept secret. To be sure, working on one's self through one's sexuality is also a choice to participate in, and be treated by others in relation to, collective values, since the meanings in use of coming out mentioned in Chapter 3 are criteria that lesbians and gay men use to define their collective existence. Indeed, coming out is itself *the* ethical imperative of lesbian and gay existence. As such, it is more aptly described through its meanings in use, rather than as a normative system lesbians and gays use to judge and "control" each other. As I have argued, lesbians and gay men can share an ethos—a very strong structure of existence—without relying upon moral injunctions or even coercive means of imposing it upon each other. A lesbian and gay community therefore cannot be *produced* through outing. One cannot be forced to enter into a process of becoming—an ethos consists in freely chosen responsibilities as well as opportunities; as the old adage goes, You can lead a horse to water, but you can't make it drink. Outing is best conceived as a political strategy rather than, categorically, a "gay/lesbian issue" (all closeted lesbians and gays should be outed). If one is engaged in homoerotic sex secretly, considering our historical context of heterosexism and homophobia one has an ethical responsibility, a responsibility to oneself, to come out. It is arguable whether someone like Malcolm Forbes should be threatened with outing unless he or she contributes as much to the community as he or she benefits from it (in the sense of using community institutions in order to be able to have sexual relationships). However, if one is currently engaging in or has in the past engaged in homoerotic sex, and one wages war against the lesbian and gay community or is purposefully indifferent to the waging of war by others when one could make a palpable difference, members of that community have the political right to defend themselves by, at the very least, exposing the hypocrisy.

(Examples of this latter case include such people as the late leader of homophobic conservatism, the closeted Terry Dolan, and the alleged closeted lesbian and gay male clerks to that Supreme Court justice who claimed, while voting with the majority in *Bowers v. Hardwick,* that he did so in part because he had never knowingly met a lesbian or a gay man.) Thus, outing is best conceived as a strategy of ensuring accountability among policymakers (broadly conceived) or public figures. Such a person's sexual orientation could *become* a "lesbian and gay issue" if her or his policies or public pronouncements had a negative impact on lesbians and gay men, in which case outing might be a significant way the affected constituency could attempt to shape policy or public opinion.

An ethos of lesbian and gay existence, then, is a basis for a political ontology and epistemology. As an ontological source of politics, this ethos is a self-disclosure, a public creation of the self in coming out. It is also the identification of one's freedom to do so—indeed, one's personal destiny—with that of other gay men and lesbians, the lesbian and gay community. This conceptualization of coming out also places limits on the possibility of politics. Politics is limited by the fact that one cannot force another to be free, to come out. Remaining in the closet and thereby acceding to domination by heterosexism and, ultimately, to subjection by homophobia is a personal ethical choice too, just as is that of coming out. Since coming out as such is a personal ethical choice, made freely and deliberately, the existence of lesbian and gay people as a people, a *community,* and the possibility for individual lesbians and gay men to come out and become gay or lesbian, are limited by the freedom of each other individual to decide for her- or himself whether to come out and become lesbian or gay. The ontological possibility of a lesbian and gay community is limited by the extent to which lesbians and gay men come out into it.

Again, its ontological possibility is conditioned by the extent to which lesbians choose to form themselves as subjects through participation in institutions that include gay men, or, in separatist fashion, through the institutions of the (lesbian and nonlesbian) women's community. It is also conditioned by the extent to which people of color choose to come out through participation in the lesbian and gay community, as distinct from through their racial and ethnic communities of birth, being "out" publically within and identifying themselves primarily as members of those latter communities. This could involve *both,* as a friend of mine wrote: "To be myself: to be Black among White gays, to be gay among Blacks."[37] But what is indispensable to be underscored is that what I have been analyzing here are the *conditions* for lesbian and gay community, which can then allow for the *emergence* of a shared ethos, or way of life, which then makes possible individual *choice* to participate

---

37. The friend cited is Robert E. Penn. This quotation is from his essay in Mark Blasius and Shane Phelan, *We Are Everywhere: An Historical Sourcebook in Gay and Lesbian Politics* (New York: Routledge, 1995). For a discussion of the tensions between understanding oneself as a black gay man or as a gay black man, see Essex Hemphill, ed., *Brother to Brother* (Boston: Alyson, 1991). For an analogous discussion from the perspective of women of color, see the relevant essays in Barbara Smith, ed., *Home Girls: A Black Feminist Anthology* (New York: Kitchen Table, Women of Color Press, 1983); and Carla Trujillo, ed., *Chicana Lesbians* (Berkeley: Third Woman Press, 1991).

in and adapt that way of life as one's own. This choice then informs all of one's other decisions in life and becomes *ethics.*

Lesbian and gay ethics, again, derived from an erotics that decenters genital sexuality and de-essentializes gender, as its effect removes sexual-affective relations from the domain of truth telling. It was on this basis that sexuality had been constituted as compulsory heterosexuality. With this truth regime displaced as the foundation for erotic relationships, the possibility of a different relational ethic emerges: reciprocity—again, lesbian and gay erotic practices involve integrating the pleasure of the other into one's own pleasure. And since lesbians and gay men need not look for their "other half" to complete themselves, within lesbian and gay sexual ethics it is not a question of having to choose between being in a couple or "promiscuity" or even being in an "open relationship." Rather, the love one feels in a domestic relationship can be different from the love one feels in purely sexual relationships that can be different still from the love one feels in friendships that may or may not involve a sexual component. Yet, the concrete practices (and challenges therein) through which one makes all these forms of love part of one's life—through relationships that are individually modulated, different in kind, and varying in intensity—are characteristic of the rich relational world that is lesbian and gay existence today.

This characteristic relational problematic within lesbian and gay life is what I have called erotic friendship. Erotic friendship is characterized by reciprocal *independence* (not interdependence based upon complementarity): the relationship has no other support than the willingness of the partners to remain in it. Such relationships are politically significant: while they do not "dissolve" the possibility of an interpersonal power relationship, and even though they exist in the social context of more or less institutionalized power relationships, they are not themselves power relations—indeed, they consist in the *limit* of power relations. In erotic friendship, because it is based upon the *reciprocal* giving and receiving of pleasure, the power to shape the other is limited by the freedom of that other to remain in or leave the relationship. To be sure, the relationship could *become* a power relation, if one party becomes dependent upon the other or the reciprocity within the relationship disappears.

Friendship has often been considered a source of politics; what is new is erotic friendship, its making permeable the distinction between sociality and sexuality. As such, erotic friendship becomes a reason for, as well as a limit to, political life. It is a reason *for* because, as Aristotle suggests, friendship consists in community.[38] Politics arises from the lesbian and gay ethos of self-invention through erotic friendships within the lesbian and gay community and consequent concern to preserve the community that makes this possible.

Further, erotic friendship is a *limit* to political life in that friendship is a relationship of reciprocal independence, equality. Lesbian and gay erotics makes pos-

38. Aristotle, *Nichomachean Ethics*, trans. Martin Ostwald (Indianapolis: Bobbs-Merrill, 1962), 1159b31–32.47. For a perspective on gay male friendship and politics, see Edward Carpenter, *Selected Writings*, vol. 1, *Sex* (London: G.M.P. Publishers, 1984); for a lesbian perspective see the works of Lillian Faderman, generally, and most recently, *Chloe Plus Olivia*, ed. Faderman (New York: Viking, 1994).

sible the creation of individual agency beyond the dependence of sex-gender complementarity and lack, which may be characterized as an invented autonomy, a new ethic. Erotic friendship is an ethico-erotic relationship productive of equality; the participants (whatever they name themselves—lovers, exlovers, fuckbuddies, partners, etc.) are inventing themselves and become the conditions for such self-invention of each other. However, they are inventing themselves according to aesthetic criteria (criteria of what pleases their intimates and their intimates' circles of intimates), not according to criteria derived from so-called truth about human nature of the sexed and gendered body. But lesbian and gay erotics is also the creation of *agency* within and through the power relations that are constitutive of compulsory heterosexuality; as such, those power relations are changed. The claim for a relational right does just that: on behalf of the creation of one's own selfhood—individuality—both the *relations* of power and the *domains* of its exercise within social life can be limited. Constituting and reconstituting oneself through erotic relations and a way of life, or ethos, with others thus allows for the emergence of a new ethic—an invented autonomy like the drag queen's assertion "I am what I am"—and a consequent new relationship of the self to politics.

This new ethic and the creation of a new relation of the self to politics—what I have termed "lesbian and gay ethos" and others have termed "queer" or "queerness"—corresponds to the development of sexuality as a concept for political philosophy. However future historians of ideas settle on a general concept, and Freudian discourse notwithstanding, *sexuality* has become a *political* category largely because of the lesbian and gay movement and the reflections of lesbians and gays upon their individual and collective existence. Sexuality, as I have demonstrated, is a technology of government: it constitutes techniques through which power has come to be exercised on behalf of truth—compulsory heterosexuality—but that power is also limited in erotic friendship. Lesbians and gays create themselves as agents through at once "discrediting" the truth claims of compulsory heterosexuality while, in creating themselves ethically, they remove their relations of sexuality from those truth claims and the power exercised on their behalf. Thus, while sexuality may have for a long time been a site where *power* is exercised, it is primarily lesbians and gays who have made it a category for *political* analysis and struggle. Beyond the lesbian and gay transvaluation of values that have been historically enforced through sexuality (including the possible transformation of that category itself into "erotics"), political philosophy can focus upon the reciprocity of erotic friendship, the constitution of ethical agency through it and the effect of this upon power relations—thus, politics. This is reflected, as I have tried to demonstrate, in lesbian and gay conceptualizations of the political.

Conclusion

In problematizing the political ontology (sexual dimorphism) and political epistemology (reproductive complementarity) of compulsory heterosexuality as it is enforced through sexuality as a technology of government, lesbians and gays produce political knowledge. What can be conceived as political for lesbians and gays are all the power relations that keep them from coming out, from becoming lesbian or gay through living what I have called a lesbian and gay ethos. The ethos problematizes and displaces the regime of truth that grounds all human relationships in a male/female binary and a necessary link between erotic role, social role, and the organization of society, that has been institutionalized as "sexuality" through medicine and psychiatry or psychology, for example, and that then authorizes the exercise of power on behalf of such expertise through law, education, and other means. These power relations are endemic within everyday life through procedures of subjection and the forms of domination that support them. (Another example: lesbians and gays have, through AIDS activism and patient self-help and empowerment, problematized domination over people's bodies by medical power, and its corresponding subjection through the doctor-patient relationship, as well as the direction of the medical research agenda itself.)

Thus, the categories of political cognition that I have elaborated throughout are all attempts to make comprehensible the experience of lesbians and gays as political: domination (by heterosexism); subjection (homophobia, including gay/lesbian "self-hatred" or psychological "colonization"); erotics and the formation of political subjectivity; the relational right; the concept of "gay and lesbian community" in both its local gemeinschaft and wider gesellschaft dimensions, giving rise to a lesbian and gay public sphere; and my formulation of a lesbian and gay way of life—ethos—that gives rise to politics and of coming out into it as an ethical choice that implies other ethical choices. This politicalness is conditioned by the historico-temporal character of compulsory heterosexuality—the institutionalized power relations that constitute heterosexism and promote homophobia—as well as by the spatial dimensions of its public sphere. As such, conceptualizing lesbian and gay existence as an ethos understands what I called, at the outset of my analysis, a *historical* ontology of politics. The possibility of politics is conditioned by the historical character of the political action lesbians and gays engage in (and, indeed, the categories "lesbian" and "gay" are themselves historical). Its possibility is also conditioned by the historical emergence of a public sphere—"the lesbian and gay community"—within which lesbian and gay people can appear to each other, debate, and act, making possible a "we" of acting together.

In problematizing sexuality as a technology of government through its emerging ethos, lesbians and gays have created a transnational public sphere within which action around the power relations that constitute sexuality has become possible. Such political action affects state policies but is not purely statist in orientation. Rather than being concerned with such merely constitutional issues as how power relations are codified by the state, lesbian and gay politics has been concerned with more broadly constitutive issues—*How* shall we live? What *is* our lesbian and gay way of life—our ethos—and what is it worth? This has been the focus of their politics, just as the character of human life on the planet becomes the substance of politics generally because of the historical ascendance of biopower. The emergence, therefore, of lesbian and gay ethical subjectivity and agency as an art of living through one's erotic relations introduces something historically new onto the political landscape.

Index